D1093831

Fanny Elssler in her dressing room at the Park Theatre, New York, 1840.

Oil painting by Thomas Sully after Henry Inman

IMAGES OF THE DANCE

Historical Treasures of the

Dance Collection 1581–1861

by Lillian Moore

The New York Public Library

Astor, Lenox and Tilden Foundations

New York

THE DANCING SCHOOLE.

1 *A seventeenth-century dancing school*

A book or a print that belongs to a great public library takes on a special vitality, almost a life of its own. Though it be of the greatest rarity and value, it is seldom permitted to languish very long under glass. It is used. Savored by active minds, scrutinized by eager eyes, it provides stimulation and inspiration; the polished product of the writer or painter is transmuted into the raw material of fresh creation.

The Dance Collection of the New York Public Library is a center for such magical activity. Fortunate in its subject, an art and pastime of the deepest cultural and social significance, it has expanded with spectacular rapidity. Since its inauguration by Dr Carleton Sprague Smith in 1944, it has grown from a small corner of the Music Division to the achievement of Division status on its own, probably the first such dance section in any public library. This extraordinary development would have been impossible without the tireless enthusiasm of its Curator, Genevieve Oswald, the generosity of its many donors, and the encouragement of the Library's farsighted Administration.

In the course of its growth, the Dance Collection has strengthened its resources to a phenomenal extent. The dance is a visual art, so its pictorial records are of primary importance. To an ever increasing degree, as the needs of its users have been clarified, it has acquired prints, photographs, and illustrated books on every conceivable aspect of its subject. In the course of building up a collection which would serve both the professional and the layman, the Division has amassed a store of treasures to delight the most fastidious connoisseur.

The period 1581–1861, covered in the present book, is rich in handsome delineations of the dance, in luxuriously illustrated books and fine prints. However, most of these highly desirable items are of the utmost scarcity. Originally issued in small quantities for a limited public, they have been reduced by the vicissitudes of time until some survive just in single examples. With a policy of constructive acquisitiveness and the help of the dance world, the Dance Collection gradually built up archives of considerable importance. At the same time, individual collectors such as Lincoln Kirstein and Walter Toscanini (donor of the fabulous Cia Fornaroli Collection) through assiduous searching had formed valuable private collections. With the addition of these splendid donations, and the generosity of the Friends of the Dance Collection, the Division has become a real treasure-house of historical material.

A touchstone of the collection is its copy of John Playford's *The Dancing Master*, on whose title page the seventeenth-century dancing school appears. The first English dance book, it was published in no less than seventeen editions between 1651 and 1728, yet because it was a truly practical book, giving music and instructions for country dances, copies were literally worn out, until now they are rarer than emeralds. The Dance Collection's copy is handsomely boxed, but the little oblong book inside is shabby and fragile. Evidently it has furnished the patterns for many a merry measure—as it still can do.

2 Ballet Comique de la Reine

Ben Jonson was nine years old when the *Ballet Comique de la Reine* was presented, in 1581. He could scarcely have seen the magnificent spectacle, given in Paris to celebrate the betrothal of the Duc de Joyeuse to Marguerite of Lorraine, sister of the Queen of France. Nevertheless he seems to have owned the beautifully printed account of it published by Ballard in the following year. His signature is scrawled on the title page of the Library's copy of the book, which is considered the first actual ballet libretto. The *Ballet Comique de la Reine* undoubtedly influenced the form of Jonson's masques, produced a quarter of a century later at the English court.

The same volume contains the bookplate of Horace Walpole, who missed seeing the Ballet Comique by two centuries, but was such an assiduous theatregoer that his famous *Letters* are peppered with references to the celebrated dancers of his time.

It was Catherine de' Medici who introduced to France the Italian custom of elaborate banquet entertainments in which classic or allegorical legends were told through entrées of dancing and music. Her director of court festivals, an Italian named Baltazarini da Belgiojoso (or Balthasar de Beaujoyeux), was responsible for the staging and choreography of the *Ballet Comique de la Reine*. Presented at the Petit Bourbon on October 15, 1581, it told the story of Circe. The lavish spectacle was enacted by professional artists and the ladies and gentlemen of the Court, including the Queen herself. It lasted from ten at night until five o'clock in the morning.

The eighteen engravings in the libretto are attributed to J. Patin, painter to the King. The first depicts the opening scene, with an actor (the Sieur de la Roche) delivering the prologue; another shows the entrée of the four virtues of Faith, Justice, Charity, and Prudence, wearing elaborate star-studded costumes and carrying symbolic emblems.

Towards the end of the sixteenth century there was very little technical difference between the social dances of the aristocracy and the dancing seen in the entrées of the court ballets. The latter had more complicated floor patterns and more formal groupings, as well as more elaborate costuming. Nevertheless the steps and positions of ballroom dances were almost identical with those used in the ballets.

The handsome dance manuals published at this period consequently reveal much about the background of the theatrical dance, although they describe the pavanes and galliards popular at the time, and the illustrations depict courtiers dancing for their own amusement. Fabritio Caroso's *Il Ballarino* originally appeared in Venice in 1581. It is this first edition which has furnished the engraving of two dancers, whose dignity and elegance are so typical of that era.

Cesare Negri, working in Milan, was strongly influenced by the Spaniards who then occupied the city. His *Spagnoletta* is a galliard, lively and gay; some of the steps and figures, as well as the position of the four dancers shown here, bear a strong resemblance to those still used in square dances. England's first Queen Elizabeth loved galliards, and the *spagnoletta* was a favorite at her court. The Dance Collection's superb copy of Negri's *Le Gratie d'Amore* is notable for its sumptuous binding (royal blue morocco exquisitely tooled in gilt), which helps to make it one of the most extravagantly beautiful books imaginable.

While Caroso and Negri were compiling their invaluable manuals at the Italian courts, their contemporary Marten de Vos was painting in Antwerp. His lusty scene, engraved by Joannes Galle, depicts a village festival and a more robust kind of dance: a strapping peasant boisterously shows off his agility as he trips over and around a cluster of eggs, presumably without breaking one.

4 Dancers from Caroso's Il Ballarino   *5 Cesare Negri's dance* Lo Spagnoletto

Egg dance

When Ferdinand II, grand duke of
Tuscany, married Vittoria della Rovere,
princess of Urbino, in 1637, the city of
Florence was the scene of fabulous
festivities which included a magnificent
equestrian pageant, or "horse ballet,"
and a musical drama, *Le Nozze degli Dei*,
which was a precursor of both opera and
ballet as we know them today.

The equestrian ballet was based on the
theme of *Jerusalem Liberated*, and it
featured very complicated choreographic
manoeuvres arranged by Agniolo Ricci
and executed by highly trained horses
and their equally skillful riders. Ricci
was an expert in the staging of such
spectacles; he had created them for the
dukes of Tuscany as early as 1615, when
he was responsible for the *Guerra d'Amore*,
given under the patronage of the Medici.
For his graceful four-footed dancers
Ricci devised evolutions as intricate and
precise as those now performed by the
Rockettes at Radio City Music Hall.
Dancing horses were once cultivated in
most of the great courts of Europe; today
they survive only in the glorious white
Lippizan stallions of Vienna, whose
thrilling performances are a living
reminder of the splendid horse ballets
of the baroque period.

The artist who immortalized Ricci's
equine choreography was Stefano della
Bella, a Florentine etcher and engraver
who was strongly influenced by Jacques
Callot. He is responsible also for the very
striking scene from the Ballet of the Sea
in *Le Nozze degli Dei*. Designed by
Alfonso Parigi and staged by the same
choreographer, Angiolo Ricci, who
directed the horse ballet, it represented a
celebration in honor of Neptune and
Amphitrite, who are seen seated in raised
thrones at the rear of the stage, while
Imeneo, cloud-borne, hovers in the sky
at the left. In the foreground are thirteen
dancers representing tritons, or sea gods.
Three of them, lightly supported by two
others, are executing steps that look
exactly like modern *entrechats*, while two

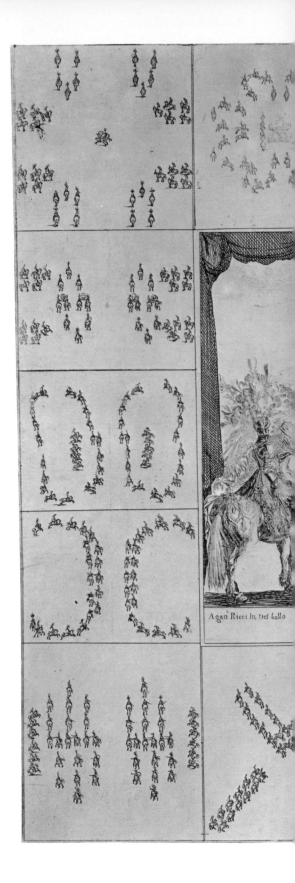

Agno Ricci In, Del ballo

7 An equestrian ballet in Florence

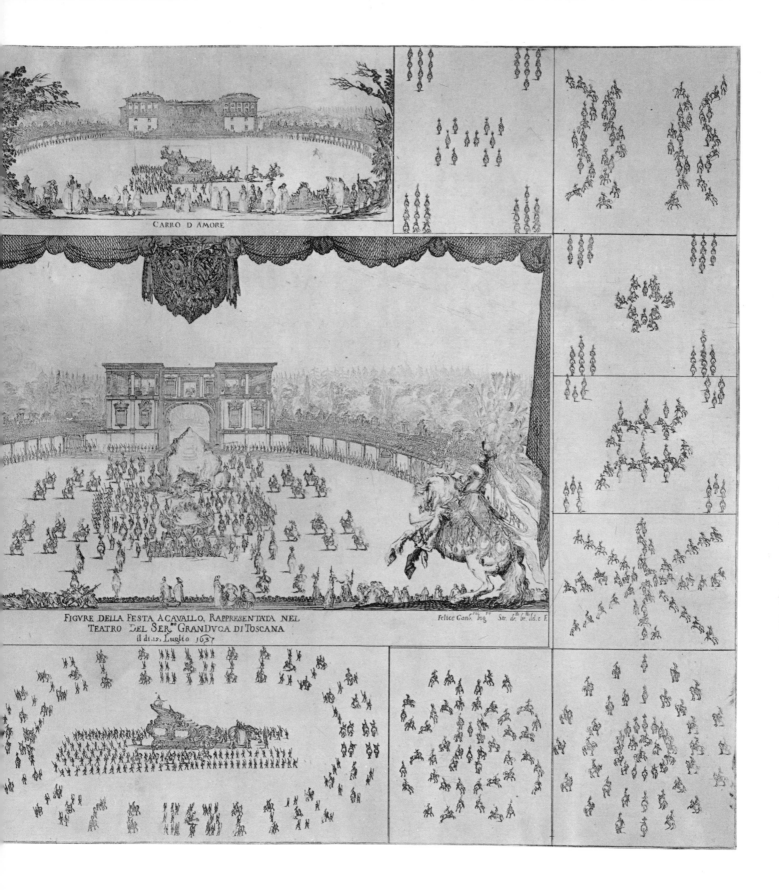

CARRO D AMORE

FIGVRE DELLA FESTA A CAVALLO, RAPPRESENTATA NEL
TEATRO DEL SER.™ GRANDVCA DI TOSCANA
il dì 15, Luglio 1637

Felice Gonfi. Ing.™   Str. s.™ br. Ild. e F.

8   Scene from Le Nozze degli Dei

more are vaulting over the backs of sea horses. Although many nobles participated in this performance, the dancers must have been professionals trained in acrobatics and the elements of what was beginning to emerge as classic ballet technique.

In France, the patronage of Louis XIV, an ardent dancer in his youth and an enlightened benefactor of the arts throughout his long life, had brought about the establishment of the Académie Royale de Danse in 1661 and the Académie Royale de Musique eight years later. These two organizations soon combined with the school for training professional dancers which Louis founded in 1672 to form the Paris Opéra, which has remained a center of ballet production and technical instruction for nearly three centuries.

In Lulli's opera-ballet *Le Triomphe de l'Amour*, in 1681, female professional dancers first appeared on the French stage. Mlle Lafontaine, the *première danseuse*, was immediately acclaimed as "the queen of the dance." Among the other participants were Charles-Louis Beauchamp, first choreographer of the Opéra, and Louis Pécourt, who was to succeed him. The theme of the ballet concerned the homage of gods and goddesses, nymphs, pleasures, and various peoples of the world to the all-powerful god of love.

Jean Berain, official designer of the Opéra, created the settings and costumes for *Le Triomphe de l'Amour*. One of the most effective was that of an Indian, a follower of Bacchus. Berain's son, also called Jean, designed the sculptor's costume for an unidentified production, about 1700. Artists of the time frequently encumbered their costumes with assorted objects associated with the profession of the character depicted. A cook, for example, might be loaded down with pots, pans, and even vegetables. Here, the sculptor's chisel is conspicuous.

Jean Berain the elder was the designer

9 *Costume for* Le Triomphe de l'Amour   10 *Costume of a sculptor*   13

11 Les Festes de l'Amour et de Bacchus

of *Les Fêtes de l'Amour et de Bacchus*, first given in Paris in 1672, and repeated at Versailles two years later. This "comedy in music" actually consisted of interludes and divertissements from several of the comedy-ballets of Molière, cleverly adapted by the composer Jean-Baptiste Lulli, so that they made one cohesive whole. The pastorale from *Le Bourgeois Gentilhomme* provided the greater part of the *Fêtes de l'Amour*, but the work also included sections of *George Dandin*, *Les Amants Magnifiques*, and *La Pastorale Comique*. Charles-Louis Beauchamp not only directed the ballets, but danced in them, while the librettist Philippe Quinault, who had collaborated with Lulli on the arrangement of the production, was responsible for its staging. The machines were constructed by the brilliant Italian theatrical architect Carlo Vigarani.

In Jean LePautre's exquisitely detailed engraving of *Les Fêtes de l'Amour et de Bacchus* it is possible to see not only the dancers on the stage and the musicians suspended and half-hidden in the trees, but the entire proscenium of the theatre at Versailles, and even the faces of some of the spectators, as well as the majestic backs of the royal party.

Lulli has been accused of taking advantage of the ailing Molière (who died in 1673) in appropriating his work and incorporating it in *Les Fêtes de l'Amour et de Bacchus*. A libretto published in 1672 did not even mention the dramatist, although his lines made up most of the text. At any rate, the lavish production consolidated Lulli's power over the newly organized Paris Opéra. *Les Fêtes de l'Amour et de Bacchus* became so popular that it was revived at intervals until 1738.

By 1700, an effective system of dance notation had been formulated and published. The author of *Choregraphie, ou l'Art de décrire la Dance* was Raoul Ager Feuillet, a dancing master who had lived in obscurity until his great work was completed. Many authorities contend

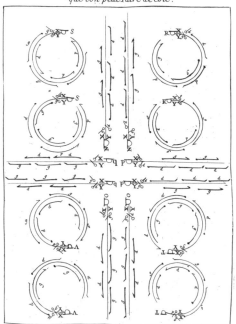

LA DANCE
*Exemples des differentes marches
que l'on peut faire de côté.*

that the true creator of dance notation was the distinguished choreographer Beauchamp, who is said to have protested the publication of Feuillet's book on the grounds that it was based on his own ideas and theories. Indeed, P. Siris, who translated *Choregraphie* into English in 1706, commented that Beauchamp had taught him its principles more than eighteen years earlier. Nevertheless, not a scrap of dance notation by Beauchamp has ever been found, and if he did actually conceive the plan for the Feuillet system he apparently preserved no written evidence of his invention.

The Feuillet choreography is decorative as well as practical, and its diagrams often have a rhythmic airy grace. The one reproduced here is notable for its spare and classic symmetry. Equally intriguing are the designs for the dance *Le Rigaudon de la Paix*, which furnish the motifs for the cover paper of this book.

Feuillet dedicated his *Choregraphie* to the ballet master Louis Pecour, many of whose dances he transcribed and published. Apparently the Feuillet system was widely used during his lifetime, for he published collections of dances, some of which had been performed by such celebrated artists as the Paris Opéra stars Jean Ballon and Marie-Thérèse Subligny, at intervals over a period of fifteen years. In England, E. Pemberton and John Weaver were prompt to publish translations of Feuillet's work.

Quite early in the eighteenth century it was introduced in Germany as well, for Gottfried Taubert devoted an impressive section of his *Rechtschaffener Tantzmeister*, one of the first German treatises on the dance, to an exposition of Feuillet's notation. In the charming frontispiece to his book, Taubert reveals his two primary interests—books and ballet—by placing his seven dancers in a library, with a backdrop of crowded bookshelves, while his "conscientious dancing master"

meditates on the theory and practice of his art. Taubert, born about 1680, was a teacher in Danzig and in Leipzig, where the *Rechtschaffener Tantzmeister* was published in 1717.

Eight years later Pierre Rameau's *Le Maître à Danser* appeared in Paris. Its illustrations were drawn and engraved by the author, who was a dancing master rather than a graphic artist by profession, so they are crude in execution but unusually authoritative insofar as the dance poses are concerned. In *Le Maître à Danser* the five positions of the feet, first definitively established by Beauchamp and still the essential base of all classical dancing, are carefully delineated. Except for the fact that in Rameau's time the turned-out position of feet and legs was not so extreme as it is today, his figures might still serve as admirable models. Rameau analyzes the steps used in the ballets and social dances of his time, many of which have survived in somewhat altered form but under the same names (*jetés, chassés, entrechats, pirouettes*, etc). He also describes the exact conduct of a formal court ball under Louis XV, with the dances following a prescribed order: first the branle, then the gavotte, and finally the most popular dance of the century, the minuet. The king was always the first to dance it. After he had resumed his place on the throne at the end of the ballroom, the prince next in rank led forward the lady of his choice. It is the charming formality of this moment, at the commencement of the second minuet, that Rameau has illustrated in the plate reproduced here.

The books of Feuillet and Rameau, like those of Caroso and Negri, are cornerstones of the Dance Collection. Both of those represented here came from the Lincoln Kirstein Collection, and have a special interest because they were the copies he used in writing his *Dance: A Short History of Classical Theatrical Dancing*, published in 1935.

12 *A dancing master meditates on ballet*

13 *Dance notation by Feuillet, 1700*

Minuet from Rameau's Maître à Danser

15 *Marie Camargo*

Rameau's contemporary, Marie Camargo, made her debut at the Paris Opéra in 1726. She received much of her early training from a man, David Dumoulin, who taught her steps such as the *entrechat* and *cabriole* which no woman had previously mastered. Thus she became the first ballerina to achieve brilliance and virtuosity as well as grace. Proud of the speed and precision of her flashing feet, Camargo daringly shortened her skirts to the middle of the calf. The height of her jumps obliged her to adopt the *caleçon de precaution* ("precautionary drawers") considered unnecessary by the dignified *danseuses* who had preceded her. Camargo is also credited with the invention of the heel-less ballet slipper, although contemporary pictures invariably show her wearing tiny heels, like the other dancers of her time.

Praised by Voltaire, Camargo was a favorite subject of the painter Nicholas Lancret. One of his portraits of her hangs in the National Gallery in Washington, D. C.; another, on which the Dance Collection's fine engraving by Laurent Cars is based, is in the Wallace Collection, London.

The basic costume of the male classic dancer, at that time, was the *tonnelet* or short, full skirt, very similar in shape to the *tutu* adopted by ballerinas more than a century later and still very much in favor. Plumes, ribbons, tassels, garlands, and rosettes were used indiscriminately to trim everything from the crisply stylized costume of the *danseur noble* who played Zephyre, shown here in the engraving by Jean Baptiste Martin, to the less formal but almost equally ornate one worn by a character dancer in the role of a Spanish peasant. It was against such sumptuous but highly improbable theatrical dress that Jean Georges Noverre made his eloquent plea for the reform of ballet costume in his epoch-making treatise, *Lettres sur la Danse et sur les Ballets,* in 1760.

In the ballrooms of the eighteenth century, the minuet reigned supreme. Its elegance, dignity, and mannered grace reflected the atmosphere of the French court, but it was equally popular in less aristocratic surroundings, and although George Bickham's *An Easy Introduction to Dancing, or, The Movements in the Minuet Fully Explained* is now a rarity, it once sold for a shilling and served as a simple "teach yourself to dance" manual. Bickham was an English engraver with a fairly extensive knowledge of several arts. He is remembered for his work on calligraphy, *The Universal Penman*, and the attractive plates of his two folio volumes, *The Musical Entertainer*.

Originally a lively rustic dance of the French province of Poitou, the minuet was danced in three-four time, and derived its name from its small, dainty steps (*menus pas*). It was a favorite of the composer Lulli, who first incorporated it in the musical suite; it is found in works of Handel and Bach, Haydn and Mozart, and Beethoven transformed it into the symphonic scherzo. The dance likewise went through many changes, while retaining its essential character.

The stately promenade of the minuet, punctuated by formal poses and precise pointings of the feet, made it almost a ritual, in which the presentation of a hand was a carefully studied and supremely gracious gesture. The high priests of the ceremony were the dancing masters, arbiters of style and sometimes —like the celebrated Marcel, who made even his royal pupils submit to his strictures—absolute dictators. Marcel had been a first dancer at the Paris Opéra. François Nivelon came from the more democratic theatrical background of the Paris fairs, Lincoln's Inn Fields, and Drury Lane. Nevertheless he was an expert on the elaborate etiquette of the minuet, and he presents it with unquestionable authority in his handsome book, *The Rudiments of Genteel Behavior*.

18 A minuet, from Bickham's treatise, 1738

19   Lady in a minuet   *20   Gentleman in a minuet*   21

The age of the minuet was also the heyday of Hogarth and other similarly caustic satirists of the social scene. It was John Collet, a prominent member of this distinctive English school, who painted *Grown Gentlemen Taught to Dance*, a devastating comment on the hopeless (but well remunerated) efforts of a dancing master to transform a clumsy oaf into an ornament of the ballroom, while another unfortunate student tries to force his feet and knees into the accepted turned-out position while he waits for his own lesson. The picture on the wall depicts the ideal to be emulated— "Madame Elastique," the personification of charm and facility.

There is little doubt that "Madame Elastique" was the dazzling star of the King's Theatre, Covent Garden, and Drury Lane, Anne Auretti, whose engraved portrait by Gérard Scotin is one of the most desirable and elusive souvenirs of eighteenth-century ballet in England. Horace Walpole was among Mlle Auretti's admirers. In a letter to Horace Mann, late in 1742, he mentioned the opera parties which he and Lord Holderness had been organizing for the performances of Auretti and La Barberina. Although Barberina was Italian and Auretti French (she came from Provence), they belonged to the same school of dancing, the vigorous and exciting one inaugurated by Camargo. Barberina, like Marie Camargo, was noted for her *entrechats*; Auretti excelled in the *pirouette* and the *gargouillade* (a complicated aerial manoeuvre which involves twirling the right foot in one direction while the left goes the opposite way). She was noted for her spirited character work, including Dutch and Polish numbers and even a "Savage Dance" in her extensive repertoire.

During most of her seasons in London, where she retained her popularity for more than twenty years, Anne Auretti was accompanied by a sister (or daughter?) named Janeton, who was

23   *A dance in Otaheite, 1777*

almost equally attractive. The Aurettis danced together in the company of David Garrick, known for his taste and discrimination in matters concerning the ballet. His wife, the former Mlle Violette, had been a ballerina before her marriage to the great actor.

It was no accident that audiences in eighteenth-century London were intrigued by Mlle Auretti's "Savage Dance." *Robinson Crusoe*, published in 1719, had been a best seller, arousing considerable curiosity about tropical islands and their exotic inhabitants. This was a period of exploration and discovery, especially in the Pacific Ocean, where the long voyages of the Frenchman Bougainville and the English sea captains Gilbert, Byron, and Cook put innumerable remote and glamorous islands on the map.

When Captain James Cook embarked on his third and final expedition to the south seas, in 1776, he took with him a young artist named John Webber, an Englishman of Swiss descent, who had studied painting in Bern and Paris, and for a single year attended the Royal Academy, London. He was only twenty-six at the commencement of the fatal voyage, which ended in disaster when Cook was murdered by natives on the beach at Kona, Hawaii, in 1779. Webber witnessed the event, and made it the subject of his most famous picture.

Before the tragedy, however, the expedition had visited many other islands of the Pacific. It was at Tahiti (then known as Otaheite), in 1777, that Webber recorded the seductive dance which had been presented in Cook's honor, on the command of the native chief, Otoo. Tahiti had been discovered by Bougainville in 1767, and evidences of European influence were already discernible in the elaborate costumes worn by the dancers, although their rippling arms and swaying hips betray the fact that Polynesian dances at that period bore a recognizable relationship to those still preserved today.

Cook's visit to Tahiti was the subject of a ballet as early as 1789, when Antonio Muzzarelli's *Il Capitano Cook all'Isola degli Ottaiti* was produced at the Teatro alla Scala, Milan, with Pietro Angiolini in the cast. More popular, however, was the "grand serious pantomime" *The Death of Captain Cook*, first given at the Théâtre de l'Ambigu Comique, Paris, in 1788, and reproduced with enormous success at Covent Garden, London, early in the following year. *The Death of Captain Cook* reached American shores in 1793, when the Old American Company presented it at the John Street Theatre, New York. A superior production, insofar as the dancing was concerned, was undoubtedly that given in Charleston a year later, when the cast included Jean Baptiste Francisquy, Alexander Placide, Mme Placide, and Master Louis Duport.

Another navigator who caught the imagination of dramatists and choreographers was the Comte Jean François de La Pérouse, whose mysterious disappearance in the course of a voyage around the world in 1788 was later discovered to have been caused by a shipwreck on the reefs at Vanikoro, in the Santa Cruz group of the Solomon Islands. His adventures were the theme of a pantomime produced in London in 1801, and later reproduced all over Europe and America.

Webber's print of *A Dance in Otaheite* has contributed to the creation of a ballet in comparatively recent years. The Dance Collection's copy formerly belonged to Lincoln Kirstein, who commissioned Eugene Loring's ballet *Yankee Clipper* in 1937 for the American Ballet Caravan, of which he was director. Although the costumes were designed by Charles Rain, that worn by the ballerina Marie Jeanne in the Tahitian sequence was directly inspired by Webber's engraving.

While hardy explorers were boldly enlarging the horizons of civilization, Louis XV and his current favorite, Mme de Pompadour, reigned over a court where the most prodigal extravagance was merely the order of the day. During the carnival season of 1763, Versailles was the scene of a whole series of balls enlivened by elaborate and carefully rehearsed entertainments. The climax of one such fête, that of February 8, has been delineated in an engraving by F. N. Martinet after M. A. Slodtz. Given on the orders of the Duc de Duras, first gentleman of the King's chamber, the ball was directed by Papillon de la Ferté, who in his capacity as comptroller of the *menus-plaisirs du Roi* exerted considerable power over the affairs of the Paris Opéra as well as those of the court.

In his journal, M de la Ferté described this as one of the most lavish balls of the winter. The ballroom was decorated with festoons of flowers held in place by clusters of diamonds, while the chandeliers were suspended by floral garlands interwoven with jewels. Two ballets were performed, but no professional dancers appeared; the participants were the noblest ladies and gentlemen of the court. *Les Élémens*, which included entrées for Earth, Air, Fire, and Water, was so much admired that it had to be repeated. So did *La Noce du Village*, in which the Prince de Condé danced the role of the bridegroom and the Marquise de Duras that of the bride. The Duc d'Orléans played the lord of the village, the Duchesse de Mazarin his lady. The charming maypole dance depicted in the engraving was probably part of the wedding celebration.

Among the pampered courtiers at Versailles, Papillon de la Ferté probably encountered no one so difficult to handle as the temperamental Gaetan Vestris, undisputed star of the Opéra and the greatest dancer of the day. His preposterous vanity led Vestris to declare that the century had produced only

24 May Ball at Versailles

JASON ET MEDEE   BALLET TRAGIQUE.

25 **Jason et Medée** (*Baccelli, Vestris, Simonet*)

three great men: Frederick the Great, Voltaire, and himself. His arrogance was matched only by the brilliance of his art. The lightness, precision, and harmonious nobility of his dancing were unsurpassed. A superb performer, he had an instinctive talent for acting which enabled him to excel in the dramatic ballets of Noverre.

Medée et Jason, created in Stuttgart in 1763, was one of the most impressive works of the great reformer, who believed that ballet should be expressive, not merely entertaining. Vestris danced in the première, supervised its first Paris production in 1770, and in 1781 had the audacity to present it in London as his own work.

Gaetan's twenty-one-year-old son Auguste, the fruit of his liaison with the ballerina Marie Allard, shared the fantastic success of that London season. Auguste was gifted with a phenomenal ability to leap and turn, an endowment which Gaetan modestly attributed to the fact that Auguste had the advantage of himself as father! The furore caused by the two Vestris was so great that before Auguste's benefit performance, when they appeared together, the House of Commons adjourned so that all its members might attend. That night's receipts were fourteen hundred pounds, according to Horace Walpole, who was amused that he could see the Vestris dance and still remain in his senses.

In the London production of *Medée et Jason*, Adelaide Simonet danced Medea, Gaetan Vestris played her faithless lover, and the bewitching Giovanna Baccelli was Creusa, the innocent victim of her revenge. The electrifying climax of the ballet, when the enraged Medea confronts the lovers, has been depicted by John Boydell in a stunning engraving, a jewel of the Cia Fornaroli Collection. In spite of the artificiality of their costumes and coiffures, the emotions of the protagonists fairly burn through the paper, and it is easy to understand why Noverre's ballets were so revolutionary and so moving.

Giovanna Baccelli was one of the most fascinating personalities who ever graced the London stage. A sensitive artist who could arouse an audience to pity and sympathy in a tragic role like Creusa, she was equally enchanting in the sparkling comedy of Maximilien Gardel's *Ninette à la Cour* and the classic measures of a *chaconne* or a *loure*. Her beauty captivated the Duke of Dorset, who installed her in luxury at his magnificent ancestral home, Knole, and had her painted by Gainsborough and Sir Joshua Reynolds. The Dance Collection's superb mezzotint by John Jones reproduces Gainsborough's full-length portrait.

The vivacious *pas de trois* which inspired the lively etching by Pierre Lelu was danced by three of the most popular performers of pre-Revolutionary France. Marie Madeleine Guimard had a piquant delicacy and radiant charm which enhanced every role she undertook. Passionately devoted to her art, she made it one of the glories of the Paris Opéra. Off stage, however, she was capricious and wilful, and since her protectors included several of the most influential men in France, her power was extensive. More than once she led her fellow dancers in revolt against the dictatorial directors of the Opéra.

Guimard's favorite partner was Jean Dauberval, remembered now as the choreographer of *La Fille mal Gardée*, a ballet so soundly constructed that it has survived in outline for nearly two centuries, although its original steps have been lost. Dauberval had imagination, wit, and intelligence. In his choreography he knew how to blend dancing and acting imperceptibly, so that the story flowed naturally through the movement. A performer of enormous vitality and versatility, he relished comedy roles as much as classic *pas*. He was well paired with Guimard and Marie Allard, whose outstanding characteristic was her spontaneous, joyous delight in dancing.

With the French Revolution, most of the favorites of the old regime vanished into exile or retirement. New stars arose to replace them, and by 1806 even the junior Vestris, Auguste, was menaced by a younger rival, the sensational dancer Louis Antoine Duport. In that year Jean Berchoux published *La Danse, ou Les Dieux de l'Opéra*, a satirical epic poem celebrating the bitter struggle between them. The striking frontispiece depicts the defeat of the forty-six-year-old veteran, who has fallen before Duport's faultless *écarté*. Two years later, Duport relinquished his still contested position in Paris to go to Russia, where his triumphs were recorded by Tolstoy in *War and Peace*. Because his professional journey was also an elopement, and his companion the celebrated actress Mlle George, mistress of Napoleon, Duport was obliged to flee France in the middle of the night, disguised as a woman. He never danced in Paris again. Escaping from Russia just before Napoleon's invasion, he became a favorite in Naples. Eventually, as manager of the Vienna Opera, he discovered the tiny pupil who blossomed into the incomparable Fanny Elssler.

In London the principal home of ballet at this time was the splendid King's Theatre in the Haymarket, the subject of an exquisite aquatint by Bluck after Thomas Rowlandson. It clearly shows the distinctive curving apron of the stage, approved by some dancers but heartily disliked by Elssler, who, when she appeared there in the 1830s, felt that half the audience was behind her.

Ballerina at the King's Theatre from 1796 to 1807 was Mlle Parisot, whose debut created quite a stir because she was exceptionally limber, and did not hesitate to raise her legs far higher, in arabesques and other classic poses, than was customary at the time. Critics called her an "attitudinarian" rather than a dancer, but she was actually extending the boundaries of ballet technique.

30 *Duport's symbolic conquest of Vestris*   31 *Mademoiselle Parisot*

33

32   *Scene from a ballet by Viganò, 1812*

Two artists who survived the vicissitudes of the Revolution and the Empire to serve the Paris Opéra after the restoration of the Bourbons were Pierre and Marie Gardel. A contemporary of Auguste Vestris, Pierre Gardel turned to choreography early in his career, although he continued to dance and play mime parts for many years. One of his most popular ballets was *Psyché*, created for his wife in 1790, when she was still Mlle Miller. Jean Prud'hon's delicate stipple engraving shows her in this, her favorite role, which she danced until her retirement in 1816.

A choreographer of far greater consequence was Salvatore Viganò, an Italian pupil of Jean Dauberval, who developed his theories and those of his preceptor, Noverre, into a form of ballet which was powerfully dramatic. After seeing his *Mirra*, Stendhal compared Viganò to Shakespeare, declaring him a genius of equal stature. Beethoven's only ballet, *Prometheus*, was composed for Viganò.

One of his most remarkable collaborators was Alessandro Sanquirico, who designed the scenery for most of the monumental works Viganò produced at the Teatro alla Scala, Milan, from 1811 until his death ten years later. Sanquirico well understood the heroic and primitive themes which inspired the great choreographer, and translated them onto canvas with a sweeping simplicity. One of the first settings Sanquirico provided for Viganò was that of *L'Alunno della Giumenta, ossia Ippotoo Vendicato*, in 1812.

The late Cia Fornaroli and her husband, Walter Toscanini, ardent believers in the principles advocated by Viganò, assiduously collected materials concerning the work of their great compatriot. The handsome Sanquirico aquatint comes from their Viganò archives, which have enriched the Dance Collection to an immeasurable extent, and have, through microfilms, been disseminated to many other libraries.

During the Empire, the quadrille had supplanted the minuet as the most favored of ballroom dances. Since the days of Caroso and Negri there had been social dances in which couples advanced and retreated, turned their partners and circled around each other. The quadrille of the early nineteenth century was danced in a square formation. It had five set figures: the *Chaîne Anglaise* (later called *le Pantalon*), *L'Eté*, *la Poule*, *la Pastourelle*, and *la Finale*. The steps were complicated ones, borrowed from the classical ballet. A pattern of *chassés* and *assemblés* called the *pas d'été* gave its name to the second figure, glimpsed here in Lebas's graceful engraving of four couples in a quadrille.

Other steps demanded in a properly executed quadrille were the *jeté, balancé, coupé*, and *changement de pied*, while an expert would occasionally show off his dexterity with a neatly crossed *entrechat-quatre*. Such intricacies required instruction and practice. The dancing school not only prospered; it subjected its aristocratic pupils to the same artificial instruments of torture employed at that time by professional dancers: the grooved box which forcibly wrenched the feet into a turned-out position, and the frame of hinged boards which did the same for the knees and thighs. This device is shown at the left of the delicately satirical drawing of an *académie de danse* by an anonymous but keenly observant artist. As he instructs a lightly clad young lady, the dancing master, his powerfully developed calf muscles bulging, scrapes away at his tiny *pochette*. Until piano accompaniment was adopted late in the century, this little pocket violin was the indispensable aid of all dancing teachers.

The most celebrated of ballet pedagogues, Carlo Blasis, formulated his theories before he was twenty-five. His *Traîté Elémentaire, théorique et pratique de la Danse*, published in 1820, is one of the keystones of dance literature. In it

35 *A French dancing school*

36 *Four couples dancing a quadrille*

he clarified the fundamental principles of classical theatrical dancing, and established the positions which are still the basis of ballet training today.

Born in Naples in 1795, Blasis in his youth danced in Marseilles, Lyon, Bordeaux, and other cities of France. After a brief term in Paris he went to Milan, where he worked directly under Salvatore Viganò. A man of broad general culture, Blasis wrote extensively on such varied subjects as music, drama, and history. An avid student of painting and sculpture, he was also well versed in the literature of several nations, and thoroughly grounded in musical composition. In spite of the range of his knowledge, he seems to have lacked the creative imagination which makes a great choreographer. Although he produced ballets for nearly half a century, from 1819, when he choreographed *Il Finto Feudatorio* at La Scala, Milan, until 1864, when he staged several works in Moscow, it was as a teacher and theoretician that Blasis won enduring fame.

In 1837, following a severe leg injury, Blasis and his wife Annunciata Ramaccini accepted the directorship of the ballet academy at La Scala. There they trained such stars of the romantic ballet as Amalia Ferraris, Flora Fabbri, Sofia Fuoco, Giovanna Ciocca, and Marietta Baderna. Established luminaries, including Fanny Cerrito, Carlotta Grisi, Carolina Rosati, and the American ballerina Augusta Maywood, profited from his lessons whenever their professional engagements brought them to Milan.

His comprehensive artistic education had given Blasis practical training in the graphic arts, and he himself was responsible for the little drawings which illustrate his *Traîté Elémentaire*. Notable for their clear-cut simplicity, they are definitive representations of the classic ballet positions. Those illustrated here show an extension in the second position with the leg at hip level (as it is used in

Fig. 1.   Fig. 2.

Fig. 3.   Fig. 4.

38 Classical poses from Theleur's Letters on Dancing

the *pirouette à la seconde*, for example) and three variations of the *effacé*, with the arms used in different ways.

In 1831, in London, an obscure and rather mysterious dancing teacher named Theleur (possibly a Frenchification of plain Taylor) published an attractive little book called *Letters on Dancing*. Some of its illustrations proclaim him as a follower of Blasis, for they consist of separate poses from the Italian master's *Traîté* arranged in novel combinations.

Such a group is one based on the variations of the *effacé* as drawn by Blasis. Theleur has put them together to form a decorative little theatrical composition, embellished, in the typical taste of the time, with scarves and garlands.

Theleur was a curious and rather pathetic individual. After the appearance of his book he began to fancy himself a great dancer as well as a theoretician. Although he was about fifty, he turned up at the Paris Opéra and applied for the position of *premier danseur*. Not surprisingly, he was turned down. However, the hardened professionals of the Opéra were not above a little fun at his expense. He had been given the freedom of the theatre, perhaps in recognition of his position as an author. The Opéra dancers amused themselves by encouraging his delusions, hailing him as "*le grand Theleur*," and permitting him to pick up the check at their after-theatre suppers. They even persuaded him to rent the Théâtre des Folies-Dramatiques for a special performance, where he made a grand entrance in a chariot drawn by two imitation tigers—his efforts to borrow live ones from the Jardin des Plantes having proved unsuccessful—and danced a *pas seul* with roses in his hair. Apparently he never suspected that his triumph was a spurious one, and that the Opéra dancers were choking with laughter as they pelted him with flowers. But his *Letters on Dancing* survives.

39

Exotic locales continued to stimulate the choreographic imagination. Giovanni Monticini used the discovery of Florida as the subject for a ballet given in Turin in 1803, while Jean Coralli, remembered now for *Giselle*, which he staged more than a quarter of a century later, produced a work called *The Incas* in Vienna in 1807. When William Barrymore, stage director of Drury Lane, the Royal Coburg, and other London theatres, was invited to produce a grand pantomime at the Teatro alla Canobbiana, Milan, in 1825, he chose for his theme the shipwreck of the French explorer LaPérouse, and presented what was probably a fairly close reproduction of the work which had been familiar on the London stage for twenty years. Alessandro Sanquirico, whose collaboration with Salvatore Viganò had been so fruitful, designed the superb settings for *Il Naufragio di La Perouse*. The one shown here is from a very fine aquatint by Carolina Lose.

Barrymore remained in Milan for a season, producing another pantomime, *Don Giovanni, ossia Il Dissoluto Punito*, early in 1826. Returning to London, he spent several years at Drury Lane before emigrating to America, where he remained for the rest of his life. His wife, the lovely Ann Adams Barrymore, was a popular performer in the graceful English style of dancing, which emphasized lyricism and femininity rather than technical prowess. She was especially admired for her performance as Fenella, the dumb girl of Portici, in Auber's opera-ballet *Masaniello*. She danced the role often in Boston, where the Barrymores settled not long after their arrival in the United States. After her retirement from the stage Mrs Barrymore opened a dancing school where she trained several accomplished American dancers, including Fanny Jones and Cecilia McBride.

The glamor, zest, and excitement of the Spanish dance have always made it a subject appealing to painters. This is one of the reasons why the Dance Collection, which makes a conscious effort to obtain full pictorial representation of ethnic as well as theatrical and social dances, is so rich in prints pertaining to the dances of the Iberian peninsula. A prime example is the aquatint of the bolero by T. Clark after William Bradford. Undated, it probably precedes the period when Fanny Elssler, with her dashing Cachucha, made Spanish dancing such a vivid and seductive element of the romantic ballet.

A charming print, which is also a document of enormous importance in the history of theatrical dancing, is the lithograph depicting Amalia Brugnoli and Jean Rozier in *Die Fee und Der Ritter*, choreographed by Armand Vestris and produced in Vienna in 1823. This picture is significant for two reasons: it is one of the first to show a ballerina supported by her partner in an adagio movement, and it portrays Brugnoli standing on the very tips, or pointes, of her toes. Pointe work was not the sudden invention of a single person. Since about 1800, perhaps even earlier, ballerinas had been rising higher and higher on the half pointe, until they discovered that it was possible to maintain the balance for brief poses on the tips of the toes. Dancers with strong feet and a fine sense of equilibrium began deliberately to cultivate the new achievement. It is known that Geneviève-Adelaide Gosselin, Teresa Ginetti, and Fanny Bias danced on pointe before 1820, but Amalia Brugnoli was one of the first ballerinas whose fame rested primarily on her amazing virtuosity in pointe work.

Marie Taglioni, often erroneously credited with the invention of this facet of technique, saw Brugnoli in Vienna when she herself was just a novice, and always remembered the dazzling footwork of the elder ballerina. Taglioni was to make dancing on pointe something more than an acrobatic accomplishment. She

transmuted a simple feat into the symbol of poetry and romantic aspiration.

Born in Stockholm in 1804, Taglioni made her debut in Vienna at eighteen. Four years later, she appeared in Stuttgart in her father's ballet *Jocko, or The Brazilian Ape*. Taken from a pantomime which had been popular in Paris in the preceding season, *Jocko* had the exotic jungle locale still so much in favor. Audiences apparently found nothing incongruous about a South American Indian dancing on the pointes of her toes. *Jocko* featured the agile antics of a man in a monkey suit, rather than the delicate art of the young ballerina.

The Dance Collection's prints of *Jocko* and *La Sonnambula* have a special value because they show the dancers in action within the stage scene, thus giving a far clearer understanding of the productions of the time than the more usual pictures of stage settings alone, or separate portraits of individual performers.

Modern ballet audiences know the theme of the sleepwalker from George Balanchine's *La Sonnambula*, originally called *Night Shadow*. The subject was used more than a century earlier, however, by the choreographer Jean Aumer, who presented his *La Somnambule* at the Paris Opéra in 1827. Enormously successful, it soon appeared in the repertoires of companies all over Europe, and even in America.

The Dance Collection's engraving shows the climax of the ballet as it was presented in 1829 in Vienna, where the young Austrian ballerina Fanny Elssler danced the title role. The major interest of the scene, although focused on the fragile figure of the sleepwalker precariously stepping along the edge of the roof, is found in the dramatic reaction of the crowd assembled below. The scene is a vivid reminder of the balletic tradition of meaningful ensemble action, employed with such a masterful hand by Michel Fokine in *Petrouchka*, and preserved today

The 1st Position

The Dancing Lesson___Pt. 1.

Pub.d by Tho.s M.cLean 26 Haymarket. Aug.st 1.st 1835.

Etch.d by G.Cruik.nk

The Minuet.

The Dancing Lesson___Pt. 2.

Pub.d by Tho.s M.cLean 26 Haymarket. Aug.t 1.st 1835.

G. Cruikshank fec.t

44   44, 45, 46, 47   The Dancing Lesson, *four caricatures by George Cruikshank*

L'Eté

The Dancing Lesson. Pt. 3

G. Cruikshank fec.t

Pub.d by Tho.s M.cLean 26. Haymarket
Aug.t 1.st 1835.

The Sailors' Hornpipe

The Dancing Lesson. Pt. 4

G. Cruikshank fec.t

Pub.d by Tho.s M.cLean 26. Haymarket.
Aug.t 1.st 1835.

in the Royal Danish Ballet's productions of August Bournonville's *Napoli, Kermesse in Bruges*, and *A Folk Tale*.

Britain's distinguished satirist of the social scene, George Cruikshank, found dancing a congenial subject for his facile pencil. Born in 1792, he was familiar with the minuet and lived through the heyday of the quadrille, the waltz, and the polka. All of them fell victim to his devastating wit.

Although he was an extraordinarily prolific artist, Cruikshank in his youth seems to have spent almost as much time at the theatre and in the ballroom as he did over the drawing board. He loved to dance, and kept his health and suppleness so well that he was able to do a hornpipe at eighty-three, and prance through a sword dance, over poker and tongs, a year later.

The four plates of *The Dancing Lesson* reveal his affectionate understanding of the subject as well as his penetrating powers of observation. The extremely turned-out feet of both master and small pupil in *The First Position* show the influence of the classic ballet on social dancing as late as 1835. The youngsters of the aristocracy were still expected to acquire the artificial stance of the ballet dancer, even if it necessitated standing with one's feet in a box, like the plump little sufferer in the background of Plate 2, or forcing one's shoulders back by grasping a board, as in Plate 4. They learned the minuet, although it had long been a museum piece, and the enduring *pas d'été*. The boys, at least, could occasionally relax with a hornpipe.

By this time, however, it was the waltz which ruled the ballroom. Although he ignored it in *The Dancing Lesson*—perhaps because his small subjects were too young for its voluptuous measures—Cruikshank had a particular predilection for the waltz, and enjoyed sketching it in its more rowdy and athletic manifestations.

Anais Colin saw the waltz in quite a

different light, and in Sorrieu's lithograph from his drawing of the *valse à trois temps* the gentle and modest demeanor of the dancing couple would certainly have earned the approval of Queen Victoria herself. As a matter of fact, the young Victoria was very fond of dancing, both in the ballroom and on the stage. She even collected ballet prints, several of which now belong to the Dance Collection.

Queen Victoria's favorite ballerina was Marie Taglioni, whose dancing was distinguished by its ethereal and spiritual quality. Her art found its most perfect expression in her father's ballet *La Sylphide*, created at the Paris Opéra in 1832 and performed in London that same year. *La Sylphide* was the very essence of romanticism. This fresh and vital spirit had made itself felt earlier in the century in music, painting, and poetry. *La Sylphide* marked the beginning of its ascendancy in the art of the dance. This was the first of the *ballets blancs*, those "white ballets" in which exquisitely delicate creatures in diaphanous bell-shaped skirts float with imponderable lightness in moonlit landscapes. Examples popular today are the second act of *Giselle, Les Sylphides* (Michel Fokine's tribute to the romantic period), and, of course, *La Sylphide* itself. Preserved for more than a century in the repertoire of the Royal Danish Ballet (in a version by August Bournonville), it has been produced in the 1960s by Ballet Rambert, the American Ballet Theatre, and the National Ballet of Canada. Unlike its fragile heroine, it seems destined for immortality.

The story of *La Sylphide* concerns a young Scotsman, James, who falls in love with a spirit of the air. Taglioni's miraculous dancing of the title role, in which her delicate pointe work gave the actual illusion of flight, was the inspiration of countless painters and sculptors. The ballet's opening tableau, with the Sylphide kneeling beside the

sleeping James, was painted by Georges Lepaulle, and promptly reproduced by the American lithographers Edmund B. and Elijah C. Kellogg of Hartford, Connecticut, in a print which is now one of the rarest in the Dance Collection.

The scene a moment later, when the Sylphide hovers behind James's chair, is the first in a series of six lithographs based on paintings by the English artist Alfred E. Chalon. Assembled in a handsome portfolio, they were issued together in 1845 to commemorate Taglioni's first farewell performances in London. (She did not actually retire until 1847.) The second of the Chalon lithographs shows the Sylphide in the window, mourning James's bethrothal to his childhood sweetheart, Effie. In another, she is poised so lightly on the tips of her toes that she really seems to be supported by her gossamer wings. In a fourth, having persuaded James to desert Effie and follow her into her forest domain, she pauses on a slender branch to show him the nest of a bird, a sister creature of the air.

James is a mortal, and although the Sylphide loves him she constantly flies from his human grasp. An evil witch gives James a magic scarf with which to ensnare her. When he twines it around her shoulders, her wings drop off and she dies. The two final pictures show the falling of the wings, and Taglioni's gracious acknowledgement of the ovation which invariably followed her performance in *La Sylphide*.

As the most celebrated dancer of her century, Taglioni inspired dozens of painters and lithographers, but none succeeded in suggesting the imponderable lightness of her dancing more effectively than Chalon in this farewell tribute. Although separate prints from it turn up occasionally, the complete portfolio is rare indeed, and the Dance Collection is extremely fortunate in possessing an example of it.

50, 51, 52, 53, 54, 55 *Marie Taglioni in La Sylphide as drawn by Alfred E. Chalon in 1845*

THE CELESTE-AL CABINET.

DICKENSON.
I never felt the uneasiness of being a bachelor untill now—what I have beheld she is graceful as a Butterfly & soft under foll cast.

BUTLER.
She is well enough but I have conscientious scruples in these matters.

CASS.
This is a very strange introduction to the Cabinet when weighty matters are under discussion, but it does not become me to complain.

JIMMY O'NEAL. Door Keeper.
O' she'll bother them all by the powers faith, receipt my friend Kendal to her no scanle for a pretty woman, Sal dat, for my own sad Jimmie O'Neal.

CELESTE.
Mon General, if it is glory enough to serve under you, mai qui est in my grand satisfaction to see you, wid de Grand Cabinet of dis Grand Nation, here assemble.

GENERAL JACKSON.
Charming Creature.— I'm not fost at my prochant for pretty women. I take "the responsibility" of introducing her to the Cabinet.

KENDAL.
I wonder how the General could ever prefer the heels to the head. He never burnt that from me. Did the least hint the general needed.

WOODBURY.
She has once essayed to draw all the surplus Revenue out of the Treasury, How'st she, Mr. Money generally.

VANBUREN.
Pish pish Butler, this is not the age for scruples of any kind. I like her rapid movements, her quick changes, her graceful evolutions. She is of my school. She has patiently & most consummate votes. Trusts her to my bett knight.

Not even the incomparable Taglioni was safe from caricature. If this goddess of the dance suffered from the lampoons of satirists who made fun of her slenderness, her modesty, and her demure expression, lesser luminaries were far more vulnerable. In the United States, in particular, they sometimes suffered from the harsh ridicule they received in prints which seem merely amusing and interesting to us now, but were misleading and even cruel at the time of their appearance.

Ballet had been introduced in the United States shortly after the American Revolution. It had enjoyed a mild and intermittent popularity until the 1830s, when the advent of European ballerinas of stature, and the development of American dancers in the schools of Philip Hazard, a former member of the Paris Opéra ensemble, and Ann Adams Barrymore, a graduate of the London stage, gave the art a strong impetus. Enhanced by the newly developed technique of dancing on the pointes and the attractiveness of romantic themes, ballet gradually assumed a position of importance in the American theatre.

One of the most glamorous of the imported dancers was Mlle Celeste (born Celeste Keppler), who arrived in New York in 1827. Barely sixteen, she was a comparative novice, but her Paris Opéra training plus a brilliant talent for mime and a tremendous flair for the theatre soon made her a star of the first magnitude. One of the first to dance on pointe in the United States, she excelled in *pirouettes* and other *tours de force*, but was especially distinguished by the dramatic talent which enabled her in later years to become a first-rate actress.

It was Celeste who first brought an excerpt from *La Sylphide* to America, in 1835, but the ethereal role did not suit her robust personality, and she never danced the complete ballet here. More to her taste were such *travesti* mime roles as that of the Wild Arab Boy, where she revelled in the opportunity to play havoc with the emotions of the spectators while generously exhibiting her well-rounded legs.

During her second tour of the United States Celeste is said to have attracted the favorable attention of President Andrew Jackson, whose weakness for pretty ladies had already embroiled him in difficulties more than once. At any rate, during the presidential campaign of 1836, when Jackson's follower Martin Van Buren was running against both William Henry Harrison and Daniel Webster, the well-known political caricaturist Henry R. Robinson used an imaginary scene in the White House, with the charming French ballerina performing for the President and his "Celeste-Al Cabinet," as a form of anti-Jacksonian propaganda.

Except with the rabid minority, it probably did Celeste no harm to find her name linked with that of the President of the United States. Eugenie LeComte, on the other hand, nearly suffered professional ostracism because of the bare-bosomed "portrait" of her circulated by Robinson. Mme LeComte had enjoyed a fairly impressive career in France, England, Italy, and even in Russia before she came to America in 1837. She made her debut at the Park Theatre, New York, as the Abbess Helena in Meyerbeer's opera-ballet *Robert the Devil*, in which she led an infernal ballet of renegade nuns. It is quite certain, however, that she did not do so in the totally topless costume depicted in the Robinson print. Perhaps the whole affair of "the prosecuted picture" was instigated by a professional rival.

Mme LeComte survived the scandal to tour the country several times. It was she who brought Marius Petipa to America for a brief and unlucky season in 1839. It was a financial disaster, and the future choreographer of *Swan Lake* made only a few appearances in New York before scurrying back to Europe.

57 *Celeste as the Arab Boy*

58 *Eugenie LeComte*

The ballerina of the century, for the American public, was the glorious Fanny Elssler. She not only made a profound artistic impression—Ralph Waldo Emerson and Margaret Fuller were among her admirers—but she created a furore which found expression in all sorts of tangible souvenirs of her triumphant progress around the country. Dozens of music sheets appeared, each containing the accompaniment to one of her favorite dances and bearing her lithographed portrait on the cover. Her likeness was embossed in glass on whiskey bottles, and pressed in crude but curiously attractive little metal gilt figurines which still turn up, occasionally, in lamps or girandoles. James Varick Stout carved a life-size statue of her, and amassed a small fortune by exhibiting it for an admission fee of twenty-five cents.

Nathaniel Currier, who later formed half of the famous printmaking firm of Currier and Ives, was a balletomane and a particular admirer of Elssler's. He published more than a dozen prints and music covers depicting the fascinating artist in the Cracovienne, the Cachucha, the Zapateado and the other colorful and exhilarating dances she made so distinctly her own. One of his most successful publications (based on a European original by Lejeune) was *The Three Graces*, a blatant piece of Elssler propaganda. It places her prominently front and center, at the resplendent zenith of her career, while the aging Taglioni fades into the background and the young Fanny Cerrito turns her head covetously towards the spotlight.

Elssler was indeed at the very peak of her powers during her two-year American tour, 1840–1842. Born in Vienna in 1810, she had already conquered the discriminating audiences of Paris, Berlin and London before she came to the United States. At thirty, she was noted for the precision and virtuosity of her dancing, which encompassed pointe work more intricate than anything previously attempted. However, it was her extraordinary beauty, the eloquence of her acting, and the intoxicating warmth of her stage presence which set her apart from other dancers. She was the very antithesis of Taglioni, who danced like a disembodied spirit; Elssler was a magnificent specimen of womanhood.

During her sojourn in this country, Elssler did much to encourage American dancers. Julia Turnbull, Fanny Jones, George Washington Smith, Henry and Harriet Wells, and the four Vallee sisters all danced in her company from time to time. Unfortunately the lovely Cecilia McBride, a pupil of Ann Adams Barrymore, contracted tuberculosis and by the time of Elssler's visit was no longer able to dance. She struggled on for several years as an actress, and died in Boston, the city of her birth, in 1846. Pendleton's charming lithograph is the only surviving souvenir of her brief career.

Fanny Elssler, on the other hand, rivalled Taglioni in the number and quality of the art works she inspired. Her Cachucha was captured in an excellent bronze by Barre, now in the Dance Collection, which also has a fine bisque statuette of her in the same dance. Shortly after her New York debut, which took place at the Park Theatre on May 14, 1840, the noted American artist Henry Inman persuaded Elssler to sit for him. She posed at the theatre, seated before her dressing table, and wearing the white costume of the bridal scene in *La Tarentule*, the ballet she had danced on her opening night. Elssler was so pleased with the portrait that she took it back to Vienna with her, but before her departure she permitted a still more celebrated painter, Thomas Sully, to copy it. Perhaps best known for his handsome portrait of the young Queen Victoria, which hangs in the Pennsylvania Museum of Fine Arts, Philadelphia, Sully was a pupil of Benjamin West. The son of Matthew Sully, a popular actor-

60 *Cecilia McBride*

dancer and mime, the future painter was a dancer at the Charleston Theatre in his youth, and had his first drawing lessons from his brother-in-law, Jean Belzons, who designed the scenery there.

The Inman painting of Fanny Elssler is now in the Haydn Museum at Eisenstadt, Austria, with other mementos of the ballerina's career. (Her father was Haydn's music copyist.) Thomas Sully's version, so glowingly alive that it must be considered a superb example of that master's art, is one of the most highly prized possessions of the Dance Collection, and serves as the frontispiece to this book. With the generous cooperation of its previous owner, George Chaffee, it was acquired and presented to the Library by the Friends of the Dance Collection.

The lithograph of Paul and Amelie Taglioni, drawn by Napoleon Sarony and published by Robinson, celebrates their American debut. This performance, at the Park Theatre, New York, on May 22, 1839, was also the occasion of the first complete production of *La Sylphide* in this country. Paul Taglioni, brother of the more famous Marie, had been her partner when she danced her favorite role in Berlin and London in 1832, the year of its creation. On those occasions his German wife, born Amelie Galster, had played Effie, the young fiancée of the hero, James. More recently, however, Amelie Taglioni had assumed the title role at the Berlin Royal Opera, where her husband was ballet master and *premier danseur*.

Fragments of *La Sylphide* had been presented on the American stage intermittently ever since Mlle Celeste had introduced a solo excerpt from it in 1835. An opera called *The Mountain Sylph*, composed by John Barnett and based on the same libretto as the ballet, had enjoyed a mild success in the United States. Augusta Maywood, then only thirteen years old and known as *la petite Augusta*, had appeared in an arrangement

in which the Sylphide's role was danced and the other principal parts were sung. Several other ballerinas, including young Harriet Wells, Mme LeComte, and Augusta St James (known on the stage simply as Mme Augusta) had starred in this hybrid version. Not until the arrival of the Taglionis, however, was the original staging seen or the Schneitzhoeffer score heard in America.

In the authentic choreography of Filippo Taglioni, with which his son Paul was of course thoroughly familiar, *La Sylphide* had a triumphant success. Amelie Taglioni (who seems to have been a lyric, poetic dancer, of the same type as her sister-in-law) was praised for effortless lightness and dexterity. Paul was compared to a race horse in his clean, sinewy muscularity. Although Charles Vestris, nephew of the great Auguste, had appeared in the United States in 1829, since then there had been no male dancer to approach Paul Taglioni. His dancing was a revelation.

Once firmly established in the American theatre, *La Sylphide* retained its popularity until the Civil War interrupted the normal course of theatrical activity. Among the ballerinas who performed it were Mary Ann Lee (remembered as the first American *Giselle*), the Philadelphia dancer Henrietta Vallee, Hermine Blangy of the Paris Opéra, the Italian Teresa Rolla, and Yrca Matthias, a French dancer who earned fame in Russia.

The most illustrious Sylphide ever to dance the role in America, however, was Fanny Elssler, who arrived the year after the Taglionis completed their single summer season here. In Paris, where she had been obliged to face direct comparison with Marie Taglioni, Elssler's Sylphide had been a comparative failure. Critical observers felt, perhaps with some justification, that she was far better suited to those exhilarating character dances she performed with such vivacity. In the United States, however, her

interpretation was appreciated for its own distinctive merits. In the final scene, where the Sylphide loses her wings and her immortality, Elssler's mime was so touching that the most hardened Yankee sceptics melted in tears.

The brilliance of Elssler's dancing is vividly suggested in a lithograph by Gauci after J. Deffett Francis, which shows her in the forgotten ballet *La Volière*. The artist has caught her in motion. She seems to be turning in the air, her filmy skirts flying, a gossamer veil swirling above her shoulders, her arched feet stretching downward in a flawless position which still conveys the illusion of spontaneity.

While Elssler was invading Taglioni's territory by dancing *La Sylphide*, her rival was reciprocating by appearing as a gypsy girl in the ballet *La Gitana*, which her father had created for her in Russia in 1839. She danced the role two years later in Milan, where Roberto Focosi recorded her performance in an unusually beautiful lithograph. She seems the personification of lightness and grace. But if one took away the tambourine and added a pair of wings, she might easily appear to be dancing *La Sylphide*. The flashing eyes and voluptuous abandon of the gypsy seem to have eluded the decorous Taglioni.

In the meantime, a younger and less spiritual Sylphide had been attracting considerable attention. Her 1841 appearances in Milan had preceded Taglioni's by just a few weeks. Born in Naples in 1817, Fanny Cerrito was a sunny child of the south. She had abundant energy and a radiant smile; where Taglioni floated, she bounced. Her infectious charm made the sternest critics forget the deficiencies of her technique. Why should anyone quibble about precision and neatness when Cerrito could spin so swiftly and dart about the stage with such reckless assurance?

In London in 1842 Cerrito found a role

which suited her to perfection. In *Alma, the Daughter of Fire*, she played the part of a statue given life on condition that she never fall in love. Guided by the demon Periphete (Jules Perrot), Alma undergoes all sorts of tests before she succumbs to the ardor of the Moorish prince Emazir, and is turned back to stone. The Dance Collection's water color shows the *Pas de Fascination* in which, urged on by Periphete, the irresistible Alma enchants the entire population of a German village. Unsigned, the drawing is probably R. J. Hamerton's original for the lithograph issued by William Spooner in 1842. *Dancing in Prints*, the portfolio of reproductions published by the Library in 1964 to celebrate the twentieth anniversary of the Dance Collection, includes another fine lithograph, by Bouvier, depicting Cerrito in the same dance.

An unsolved mystery concerns the album of costume sketches which includes the design for Marie Taglioni's costume in *Herta*, a ballet her father produced for her in Russia in 1842. This particular water color bears Marie Taglioni's own autograph signature, as does one other drawing in the little book. Did it ever belong to her? A fascinating project is waiting for the right scholar, in the study of this collection of designs.

Esmeralda, based on Victor Hugo's *Notre Dame de Paris*, was a superb example of Jules Perrot's choreography, in which brilliant dancing and expressive mime were inextricably blended. Bouvier's lithograph shows Perrot dancing the *Truandaise* with Carlotta Grisi, the young Italian dancer who had recently created the title role of *Giselle*. In Grisi were united all the best attributes of the other outstanding ballerinas of the romantic period: the buoyant elevation of Taglioni, the technical virtuosity and mimic powers of Elssler, and the joyous, exuberant facility of Cerrito. If she could not claim to surpass her peers in any one aspect of her art, Grisi

65   *Costume for Marie Taglioni in* Herta   66   *Fanny Cerrito in* Alma

outstripped them all in versatility. *Giselle* gave full scope to every facet of her talent. The first act, with its mad scene, demands an actress of consummate ability; the second (where the betrayed heroine has been transformed into a Wili), a dancer capable of suggesting the imponderable lightness of a disembodied spirit. Because it requires such a consummate mastery of the whole range of classical dancing, *Giselle* is still considered the touchstone of the ballerina's art. Danced in recent years by such memorable interpreters as Alicia Alonso, Margot Fonteyn, Alicia Markova, and Galina Ulanova, the role is still indelibly linked with the name of Carlotta Grisi, for whom it was created.

Giselle was first performed at the Paris Opéra on June 28, 1841. The libretto, based on a German legend related by Heinrich Heine, was written by Grisi's ardent admirer, Théophile Gautier; the score was composed by Adolphe Adam. Jean Coralli was credited with the choreography, but he undoubtedly received considerable assistance from Perrot, who was Grisi's discoverer, teacher, and husband. Lucien Petipa created the role of Albrecht, which has been danced so nobly in our time by Erik Bruhn, Henning Kronstam, and Igor Youskevitch. The first Myrtha, Queen of the Wilis, was Adele Dumilâtre, who appeared in the same part in London two years later when Fanny Elssler, on her return from America, danced Giselle.

The clean lines of Dumilâtre's arabesque in Bouvier's lithograph graphically convey the cold, clear-cut character of the role of the Wili Queen. Dumilâtre was a dark-haired beauty who briefly challenged the recognized stars of the romantic ballet in Paris and London, without ever attaining their celestial heights. She did, however, inspire several unusually attractive prints, and Bouvier in particular seems to have found her an appealing subject.

From the ballet academy at La Scala, Milan, where Carlo Blasis and his wife

68   Adele Dumilâtre as Myrtha in Giselle, *1843*

had been teaching for some years, there began to emerge at about this time the vanguard of the long procession of Italian ballerinas who were to rule the stage for nearly half a century. They were brilliant technicians, who could perform all sorts of dazzling and previously unattempted feats on their toes. Blasis' pupils were particularly adept at pirouettes and turns of all kinds, for he had apparently discovered the trick of snapping the head at a faster rhythm than that of the body, which keeps the dancer from getting dizzy.

Blasis was especially proud "of seven dancers whom he called his Pleiades." These were Marietta Baderna, Augusta Dominechettis, Amalia Ferraris, Sofia Fuoco, Flora Fabbri, Carolina Granzini, and one man, Pasquale Borri. In his *Notes Upon Dancing*, published in London in 1847, Blasis described the individual characteristics and listed the professional triumphs of these favorites.

Among the first to acquire international celebrity was Flora Fabbri, who made her London debut at Drury Lane Theatre in the autumn of 1845, dancing the role of Mazourka, a basket maker's wife, in Joseph Mazilier's ballet *The Devil to Pay*. The part had been created by Carlotta Grisi earlier that same year, at the Paris Opéra. It required a fine sense of comedy as well as no little virtuosity, but Fabbri, in the English production, succeeded in making it very much her own. She appeared at the Paris Opéra intermittently from 1845 to 1851, and toured widely in Italy and Germany. According to Blasis, audiences were invariably entranced by the joyous and ardent spirit of her dancing.

Marietta Baderna, born in 1830, was only sixteen years old when Giuliani's unusual lithograph of her was published in Milan. It shows her surrounded by sixteen miniature figures representing her various roles. Poses from *Giselle* and *La Sylphide* are recognizable, and apparently Baderna was adept at the

70 *Marietta Baderna, 1846*

various Polish, Spanish, and Russian dances which Fanny Elssler had made so popular. For such a youthful artist, her repertoire was amazingly extensive. When Carlo Blasis accepted an engagement as guest choreographer at Drury Lane, early in 1847, he took Baderna along to interpret the leading roles in the ballets he produced there. Critics praised her lovely arms and strong pointe work. They found, however, that Blasis seemed unable to develop a dramatic theme, although he staged effective dances and divertissements.

Baderna was one of the first classic dancers to visit South America. In 1850 she appeared in Rio de Janeiro, where she was lucky enough to escape the ravages of a yellow fever epidemic which killed 16,000 people, including her own father.

The most distinguished of all Blasis' pupils was Amalia Ferraris. Her technique was prodigious. She could leap like a fawn, and descend as gently as a falling leaf. The strength of her pointe work was astonishing, and she is said to have been able to balance on the tip of one toe on the narrow side of a tambourine.

Born at Voghera, Italy, in 1830, she was a star at Her Majesty's Theatre, London, by the time she was twenty. There she competed successfully with such established artists as Fanny Cerrito and Carlotta Grisi. Later she ruled for seven years as prima ballerina at the Paris Opéra, and in 1858 made her debut in St Petersburg, where Jules Perrot produced his *Eoline* for her. The charming lithograph by Marcovich records a delightful pose (typical of the period) which occurs also in the *pas de deux* from August Bournonville's *Flower Festival in Genzano*, still danced today.

Giovannina King was not one of Blasis's "Pleiades," but she was his pupil. Her earliest training, however, was received under Pietro Hus in Naples, her birthplace, and she also studied under Bournonville's pupil Gustave

73   *A Neapolitan tarantella*

Carey. (Her pose, like that of Ferraris, is reminiscent of the Danish master.) Most of her career was spent in Italy, and she danced with enormous success from one end of the peninsula to the other. The source of her English name remains a mystery.

Sofia Fuoco, like Ferraris, was a *ballerina di forza.* Her pointe work was marvellous. She was probably one of the first dancers to turn pirouettes on pointe. In the very soft, unboxed satin slippers worn during the romantic period such a feat would have required amazing strength and control, but Fuoco seems to have accomplished it.

Born in Milan in 1830, Fuoco entered the ballet academy at La Scala when she was seven. She made her debut at the Paris Opéra at sixteen, and her triumphs there were followed by splendid seasons in London and Madrid. In Italy her dancing aroused such fanatical enthusiasm that not even a cholera epidemic, which was raging in Perugia during her engagement there in 1856, could keep people away from the theatre.

Fuoco made the national dance of her country, the spirited tarantella, an intoxicating theatrical experience, and her finest portrait is probably the lithograph by Sanesi which shows her dancing it. A shining example of this dashing Italian dance is the climax of the Royal Danish Ballet's wonderful *Napoli*, which August Bournonville produced after a visit to Naples in 1841. Perhaps he brought back to Copenhagen a copy of the enchanting little book of lithographs by Gaetano Dura illustrating the steps and positions of the tarantella, with directions for dancing it by Pasquale Chiodi. Its frontispiece shows a movement which Bournonville reproduced in the last act of his great ballet. The tarantella is still an inspiration to choreographers; George Balanchine created a sparkling one for Patricia McBride and Edward Villella in 1963. Most of the Dance Collection's superb

74 *Sofia Fuoco in a tarantella*

75   Pas de Quatre (*Taglioni, Grisi, Cerrito, Grahn*), 1845

gallery of Italian ballet prints belong to the Cia Fornaroli Collection, and were lovingly assembled by the ballerina and her husband. They were the donors, as well, of Brandard's striking picture of the memorable *Pas de Quatre* of 1845.

This unique divertissement has often been called the apogee of the romantic ballet. In it appeared four of the greatest dancers of that or any other period.

During the summer of 1845 Marie Taglioni, Fanny Cerrito, Carlotta Grisi, and the young Danish dancer Lucile Grahn were all simultaneously engaged at Her Majesty's Theatre, London. The enterprising impresario, Benjamin Lumley, conceived the daring idea of having them perform together in a single brief ballet, a *Pas de Quatre* of such brilliance that nothing remotely approaching it had ever been attempted before. Since the four stars were, of course, bitter rivals, it required diplomacy of the highest order to persuade them to agree to such an unprecedented proposition.

Agree they did, and Jules Perrot set to work to create a series of dances which would display the most scintillating talents of each ballerina, without giving predominance to any one of the four. All went smoothly until the final rehearsal, when the entire project nearly collapsed over the question of the order of the solo variations. The coveted privilege of dancing last had been given to Taglioni, by unanimous consent, and the comparatively unknown Grahn had agreed to be first. But Cerrito absolutely would not dance before Grisi, and Grisi just as adamantly refused to precede Cerrito. Lumley's arbitration of the affair produced a judgement worthy of Solomon: the eldest, he proclaimed, should of course have the preferred position. Cerrito, two years older than her compatriot, was more than a little reluctant to claim her victory!

Perrot's choreography must have been masterly, for it achieved an harmonious unity while permitting each ballerina to enjoy a personal triumph in steps exactly suited to her own individual style. At the first performance on July 12, 1845, the entrance of each dancer brought down a veritable hailstorm of bouquets, and at the final curtain the stage was all but buried under an avalanche of flowers.

The *Pas de Quatre* was danced only three more times that summer. Queen Victoria attended the third performance, and her proof copy of Maguire's well known lithograph of the ballet (after Alfred E. Chalon) has been reproduced in the Library's publication, *Dancing in Prints*. John Brandard's attractive study, shown here, is less familiar. It once decorated the cover of an excerpt from Cesare Pugni's delightful score, known today through recordings and through the reconstructions of the ballet choreographed in recent times by Keith Lester and Anton Dolin.

Lucile Grahn, youngest of the ballerinas of the *Pas de Quatre*, was born in Copenhagen in 1819. The favorite pupil and protegée of August Bournonville, she had an aerial lightness reminiscent of Taglioni. It was Grahn who created the title role in Bournonville's version of *La Sylphide*, first produced at the Royal Danish Theatre in 1836.

Bournonville ruled his company with an iron hand. Grahn, a strong-minded young woman with a will of her own, frequently clashed with him, especially after a successful debut at the Paris Opéra in 1838 had given her a taste of independence. When she wished to introduce Fanny Elssler's Cachucha at the Royal Theatre, the dictatorial ballet master was furious; when, to show off her sparkling footwork, she changed some of the steps in his ballet *Valdemar*, he made a formal protest to the directors of the theatre.

Early in 1839, Grahn obtained permission to accept a brief guest engagement in Hamburg. There her triumph was sensational. Intoxicated by

the adulation she received from the cordial German public, she applied for a prolongation of her leave of absence. When her request was peremptorily denied, she simply stayed in Hamburg anyway. A few weeks later she was dismissed from the Royal Danish Ballet. She never danced in Copenhagen again. Throughout the rest of Europe, however, her career was prosperous and prolonged. She spent her final years in Munich, as ballet mistress of the Hofoper, and when she died in 1907 she left her considerable fortune to that municipality. In gratitude the city named a street for her. Through all the vicissitudes of changing regimes, it has remained the Lucile Grahn Strasse.

Not one of the ballerinas of the *Pas de Quatre* ever danced in America, although from time to time there were active rumors of projected tours by almost all of them, and Fanny Cerrito came very close to accepting an offer to appear at Niblo's Garden, New York, in 1855. After Fanny Elssler's fabulous conquest, ballet remained for more than a dozen years one of the most powerful attractions in the American theatre. If the greatest stars failed to profit from this situation, a number of lesser luminaries surely did.

Hermine Blangy was a graduate of the Paris Opéra. Trained in its school, she had risen through the ranks until in 1840 she was dancing the title role of *La Sylphide* there. She also appeared as the Queen of the Wilis in *Giselle*. For three years she was prima ballerina at the Hofoper in Vienna, and in 1846 she came to the United States. The ballets she danced in New York, and on the tours which took her as far as Havana and New Orleans, included *La Sylphide*, *Le Diable Boiteux* (the work in which Elssler had first performed her alluring Cachucha), Perrot's *L'Illusion d'un Peintre*, and *La Fille de Marbre* (a version of *Alma*). In *Giselle* she was so successful that in 1847 she could dance it ten times in a fortnight in Mobile, Alabama, which certainly had not then attained the population of 200,000 it can claim today. During an engagement in New Orleans in 1846, she challenged comparison with the American ballerina Mary Ann Lee, who had introduced *Giselle* to the United States earlier that same year, by dancing the role in one theatre at the same time that Lee was appearing in it at another. Some connoisseurs preferred the interpretation of the Philadelphia girl, while others awarded the palm to the foreign ballerina.

The handsome portrait of Blangy is an untitled example of a lithograph by Charles Currier (brother of Nathaniel, of Currier and Ives fame) after Francis Davignon and Joseph Vollmering. It shows her in the second act of *Giselle*. The original drawing has been attributed to Davignon, who was responsible for a handful of the very finest American ballet prints, including the Dance Collection's stunning lithograph of Giovanna Ciocca.

Nathalie Fitzjames danced at the Paris Opéra with Hermine Blangy, and left it at about the same time, to tour in Italy. She was especially admired in Naples. In the autumn of 1850 she came to the United States as ballerina of an opera company directed by the noted impresario Max Maretzek, and made her debut at the Astor Place Opera House in *Paquita*, staged for her by Lucien Petipa. Although American audiences appreciated her proficiency, she was much too thin for their taste (even in Paris she had been compared to an asparagus) and they also thought her past her prime. The spring of 1851 found her in strange company, appearing in Brooklyn with a "Bloomer Troupe" which was exploiting the recently invented and decidedly audacious costume for women. The Dance Collection's lovely lithograph, with the line of the dancer's flying arabesque repeated in her diaphanous scarf, recalls her earlier career.

During her Italian engagements Fitzjames, like so many other dancers of renown, burnished her technique in the Milan studio of Carlo Blasis. If he attracted dancers from all over the world, he also disseminated them to its farthest corners. Giovanna Ciocca arrived in the United States in 1847, and promptly stirred up a hornet's nest by dancing the polka with such fascinating skill that her American partner, George Washington Smith, was no longer interested in executing the popular dance with his usual stage companion, Julia Turnbull. His refusal to do so caused a near-riot at the Bowery Theatre, where the ebullient "Bowery boys" nearly tore up the benches in protest. He was finally obliged to dance the polka four times (twice with each ballerina)!

The Bohemian polka had swept across Europe like wildfire in 1844, reaching American shores in the same year. It monopolized the ballroom, and after an enchanting version had been performed by Carlotta Grisi and Jules Perrot in London, it bade fair to take possession of the stage as well. Its hold on public favor was tenacious; in 1855 Pasquale Borri (the only man in Carlo Blasis's "Pleiades") staged a lively Redowa Polka for Pia Ricci, Henri Frappart, and Lorenzo Vienna, leading dancers of the Vienna Opera, where he was ballet master.

From Vienna, in 1845, came the *Petites Danseuses Viennoises*, a company of children drilled with such meticulous exactitude that they might be called the first "precision dancers," the predecessors of yesterday's Tiller Girls and today's Rockettes. They played guest engagements at the Paris Opéra, where the correctness of their geometrical evolutions put the resident ensemble to shame, and in London, where their winning and innocent demeanor charmed everyone, including the Queen. Their long tour of the United States, 1847 to

79 *Harvest Dance of the Viennese children*   80 *Redowa Polka*

81   *Polish Dance*

1849, brought golden rewards to their ballet-mistress-cum-manager, Mme Josephine Weiss, and to theatre owners all over the country.

One of their most effective numbers was the Harvest Dance, in which they plied small scythes and manoeuvred among sheaves of wheat. Their appearances no doubt awakened considerable nostalgia among the central Europeans who were beginning to pour into the United States in a rising flood of immigration. Print sellers were ready to capitalize on the longing for homelands by providing attractive scenes from the old countries; the vigorous *Polish Dance*, although published in Berlin, was widely distributed by the New York firm of Jacoby and Zeller.

Just such a Polish dance was to be adapted to the stage and featured, a few years later, in Leo Delibes' ballet *Coppélia*. In fact, the moment caught in the lithograph might almost be the opening of the first-act Mazurka. The enrichment of theatrical dance from folk sources still continues today.

The Italian tarantella, so often an inspiration to ballet masters, was a highlight of *L'Etoile de Messine*, the ballet with which Pasquale Borri made his choreographic debut at the Paris Opéra in 1861. Its leading dancer was his colleague and compatriot Amalia Ferraris, who found in the tragic role of the trusting and deceived heroine, Gazella, the opportunity for dramatic expression to match her phenomenal technique. The real star of *L'Etoile de Messine* was the ensemble, however, and the exceptional interest of the lithograph lies in the vivid clarity with which it suggests the entire stage picture and action.

Meanwhile another Italian, the celebrated mime and choreographer Domenico Ronzani, had brought to the United States the largest and perhaps the finest ballet company yet to arrive on these shores. Organized in Europe for the express purpose of the American

82 *Tarantella in* L'Étoile de Messine, *1861*

tour, the Ronzani Ballet had been engaged to inaugurate the new Philadelphia Academy of Music, which is still, more than a century after it opened its doors, one of the most imposing theatres in the country. The leading dancers were Louise Lamoureux and Filippo Baratti, the principal mimes Cesare and Serafina Cecchetti. Their seven-year-old son Enrico, future great pedagogue, teacher of Pavlova and Nijinsky, was on hand to play the urchin in *Il Biricchino di Parigi*.

It was Ronzani's production of Jules Perrot's *Faust* which was presented on the opening night, September 15, 1857. The Dance Collection's impressive lithograph may show a scene from this ballet. Probably used as a poster (it is very large, more than two feet in width), it conveys a graphic impression of the formal, decorative use of the ensemble and the airy brilliance of the stars.

The American tour of the Ronzani company marked one of the last noteworthy manifestations of the romantic ballet in this country. After the Civil War such spectacular shows as *The Black Crook* attracted a flurry of interest, but the emphasis had passed from poetic quality to mechanical display.

At the same time, photography was beginning to replace engraving as a means of recording the fleeting images of the dance. The daguerreotype had been invented before Fanny Elssler visited America. Increasing use of the new medium, combined with a gradual decline of interest in the dance towards the end of the century, led to a profound change in the visual records of all kinds of dancing. With the twentieth-century renaissance, as new forms evolved, new ways to capture them on paper and canvas developed. But the historical treasures preserved by the Dance Collection are more than merely beautiful and priceless souvenirs of vanished arts and social customs; they are the raw material which can stimulate and nourish fresh creation.

83 *The Ronzani Ballet*

The Illustrations

The actual image area of each illustration has been measured. The dimensions of the prints are given in inches and sixteenths of inches, height preceding width. The height of each book is given in centimeters.

Frontispiece Fanny Elssler

Fanny Elssler in her dressing room at the Park Theatre, New York. Oil painting by Thomas Sully after Henry Inman, 28×23.12. Friends of the Dance Collection. From the George Chaffee Collection

1 *A seventeenth-century dancing school*

Engraved illustration on title page of: The Dancing-Master:/ Or, Directions for Dancing Country Dances, with the Tunes to each Dance for the Treble-Violin./ The Twelfth Edition, containing above 350 of the choicest Old and New Tunes now used at Court, and other Publick Places./ The whole Work Revised and much more Correct than any former Editions./ The Dancing Schoole./ Printed by J. Heppinstall for H. Playford at his Shop in the Temple-Change, or at his House in Arundel-street in the Strand, 1703/ Price Bound 3s.6d./ [by John Playford] 10.5 cm. Purchase Fund

2 Ballet Comique de la Reine

3 *The Four Cardinal Virtues*

Engraved illustrations to: Balet Comique/ de la Royne, faict/ avx nopces de Mon-/ sieur le Duc de Ioyeuse & madamoyselle de Vau-/ demont sa soeur./ [written in ink: Presenté par gentilshomes/ et Dames: et com-/ pose/ P] Baltasar de Beavioyevlx,/ valet de chambre dv/ Roy, & de la Royne sa mere./ A Paris,/ Par Adrian le Roy, Robert Ballard & Mamert/ Patisson, Imprimeurs du Roy./ M.D.LXXXII./ Avec Privilege./ [written in ink at top right: Tanquam/ In the middle of the page: Sum Ben: Jonsonij/ At lower left, the bookplate of Horace Walpole. At lower right, the bookplate of Sir Henry Brooke] 24 cm. Drexel Collection, from the library of Horace Walpole and presumed to have been the property of Ben Jonson

4 *Two dancers from Caroso's* Il Ballarino

Engraved illustration to: Il Ballarino/ di M. Fabritio Caroso/ da Sermoneta,/ Diviso in due Trattati;/ Ornato di molte Figure,/ Et con l'Intauolatura di Liuto, & il Soprano della Musica/ nella sonata di ciascun Ballo./ . . . In Venetia, Appresso Francesco Zanetti. MDLXXXI/ 24 cm. The Astor Library

5 *Cesare Negri's dance* L › Spagnoletto

Engraved illustration to: Le Gratie/ d'Amore,/ di Cesare Negri Milanese,/ detto Il Trombone,/ Professore di ballare,/ opera nova, et vaghissima,/ divisa in tre trattati./ . . . in Milano,/ Per l'her. del quon. Pacifico Pontio, & Gio. Battista/ Piccaglia compagni. MDCII./ Con licenza de' Superiori./ 30.2 cm. Cia Fornaroli Collection

6 *Egg dance*

[on plate, at top] Has ducunt choreas, qvi bacchanalia vivunt./ M. de Vos invent. Joan Galle excud./ [below at left] 4 line poem in French [at right] 4 line poem in Dutch/ Engraving 8.15×11.8 plain, bound into a copy of: Charles Compan: Dictionnaire de la Danse . . . Paris, Cailleau, 1787. In Memory of Augustus D. Juilliard

7 *An equestrian ballet in Florence*

Figure della Festa A Cavallo, Rappresentata nel/ Teatro Del Sermo. Gran Duca di Toscana/ il di 15, Luglio 1637/ Agnol. Ricci In. Del ballo Felice Ganb.rai Ingre Ste. de.lla be.lla del e F. [at top] Carro D'Amore/ Engraving 12.11×17.5 plain. Plate from: Ferdinando Bardi, conte di Vernio: Descrizione delle feste fatte in Firenze per le reali nozze de Serenissimi sposi Ferdinand II. gran duca di Toscana, e Vittoria principessa d'Vrbino. Fiorenza, per Zanoli Pignoni, 1637. Gift in memory of Philip J. S. Richardson

8 *Scene from* Le Nozze degli Dei

Qvarta Scena di Mare/ Alfo.vs Parig.vs Inu/ S[tefano] D[ella] B[ella] Delt. e F/ Etching 7.14×11.6 plain. Plate from: Le Nozze degli dei Favola dell'Ab' Gio. Carlo Coppola rappresentata in musica in Firenze nelle reali nozze de Serenis.mi gran duchi di Toschana Ferdinando II. e Vittoria principessa d'Vrbino [Firenze 1637].Cia Fornaroli Collection

9 *Costume for* Le Triomphe de l'Amour

Habit d'Indien du balet du Triomphe de l'amour./ [on plate:] J. Berin del./ [n d] Engraving 10.2×7.6 plain. Purchase Fund

10 *Costume of a sculptor*

Habit de Sculpteur/ se vend sous les Charniers St. Innocent avec privil' du Roy/ Joan. Berin. jn. Jacob. le Pautre Sculp./ [n d] Engraving 10.11×7.5 colored. Purchase Fund

Mazurka des Salons.

11 Les Festes de l'Amour et de Bacchus

[at left] Les Festes de l'Amour et de Bacchus, Comedie en Musique/ representée dans le petit Parc de Versailles/ [center] II./ [at right] Festum Cupidinis et Bacchi, Comoedia ad perpetuum vocum/ et tibiarum cantum acta, In Hortis Versallianis./ le Pautre Sculps 1678./ Engraving 10.10×16.7 plain. Cia Fornaroli Collection

12 A dancing master meditates on ballet

Engraved frontispiece to: Gottfried Taubert/ Tantzmeisters zu Leipzig,/ Rechtschaffener Tantzmeister,/ oder grundliche Erklärung/ der Frantzösischen Tantz-Kunst,/ bestehend in drey Büchern/ . . . Leipzig, bey Freidrich Lanckischers Erben. 1717./ 20.2 cm. Cia Fornaroli Collection

13 Dance notation by Feuillet, 1700

Engraved illustration to: Choregraphie/ ou/ l'Art de De'crire/ La Dance,/ par Caracteres, Figures/ et Signes De'monstratifs,/ . . . Par M. Feuillet, Maître de Dance./ A Paris,/ Chez l'Auteur . . ./ Et chez Michel Brunet . . ./ M.DCC./ Avec Privilege du Roy./ 23.8 cm. Lincoln Kirstein Collection

14 Minuet from Rameau's Maître à Danser

Folding plate, engraving 11.12×10.13 inches, opposite p 53 in: Le Maître a danser,/ . . . Par le Sieur Rameau, Maître à danser des Pages/ de Sa Majesté Catholique la Reine d'Espagne./ Nouvelle Edition./ A Paris,/ Chés Jean Villette Fils, rue S. Jacques,/ à Saint Bernard./ M.DCC.XXXIV./ Avec Approbation & Privilege du Roy./ Lincoln Kirstein Collection

15 Marie Camargo

Mlle. Camargo./ [at left:] Fidele aus loix de la Cadence/ Je forme, au gré de l'art, les pas les plus hardis; [at right:] Originale dans ma danse/ Je puis le disputer aux Balons, aux Blondis/. Peint par N. Lancret. gravé par L. Cars./ A Paris chez l'auteur sur le quai de la Feraille a la croix des Perles. Et chez la veüve Chereau rue St. Jacques aux deux pilliers d'Or. Avec Privilege du Roy./ [n d] Engraving 16.4×22 plain. Purchase Fund

16 Costume for Zéphyre

Zéphyre./ J.B. Martin Inv. et Sculpt./ [n d] Engraving 8.14×6.14 plain. Cia Fornaroli Collection

17 Spanish peasant costume in a ballet

Danseur Pantomime dans les Ballets de l'Opera Fesant le Pas de Paisan Espagnol./ [n d] Engraving 12.2×8.3 colored. Cia Fornaroli Collection

18 A minuet, from Bickham's treatise, 1738

Engraved illustration to: An Easy/ Introduction/ to/ Dancing:/ or, The/ Movements in the Minuet/ Fully/ Explained./ . . . By George Bickham, Junior./ London:/ Printed for T. Cooper, at the Globe in Paternoster-Row; and sold/ by the Musick-Shops in Town and Country. MDCCXXXVIII./ (Price One Shilling.)/ 24.2 cm. Friends of the Dance Collection

19, 20 Lady and gentleman in a minuet

Plates to: The/ Rudiments/ of/ Genteel Behavior/ by/ F. Nivelon./ 1737./ 28.4 cm. Cia Fornaroli Collection

21 Grown Gentlemen Taught to Dance

Grown Gentlemen Taught to Dance./ Engraved after an Original Picture of Mr. John Collett, in the Possession of Mr. Smith./ Printed for Jno. Smith, No. 35, in Cheapside, & Robt. Sayer, No. 53, in Fleet Street, as the Act directs 20th Aug. 1768./ Engraving 12.5×9.12 plain. Lincoln Kirstein Collection

22 Mlle Auretti

Mademoiselle/ Auretti/ G. Scotin Sculpt./ Published According to Act of Parliament Jany. ye 15th. 1745/6/ Engraving 17.3×13.6 plain [example from the collection of Queen Victoria]. Lincoln Kirstein Collection

23 A dance in Otaheite, 1777

A Dance in Otaheite./ J. Webber del. J. K. Sherwin sc./ [at top right] 28/ Engraving 8.15×14.14 plain. Plate for: James Cook: A Voyage to the Pacific Ocean. London, 1784, II. Lincoln Kirstein Collection

24 May Ball at Versailles

Bal du May donné à Versailles pendant Le Carnaval de L'année 1763, sous les Ordres de/ M. le Duc de Duras Premier Gentil-homme de la chambre du Roi, et ordonnée par M. DeLaferté/ Intendant et Controlleur Général de L'argenterie menus plaisirs et affaires de La Chambre de sa Majesté/ Delin. M.A. Slodtz Sculp. F.N. Martinet/ [n d] Engraving 9.13×15.5 plain. Purchase Fund

25 Jason et Medée (*Baccelli, Vestris, Simonet*)

Jason et Medee [five bars of engraved music]
Ballet Tragique./ Published July 3rd. 1782 by
John Boydell Engraver in Cheapside London./
Engraving with bistre wash 14.13×18.2. Cia
Fornaroli Collection

26 *Auguste Vestris, 1781*

A Stranger at Sparta standing long upon one
Leg, said to a Lacedaemonian,/ I do not believe
you can do as much: "True (said he) but every
Goose can"./ See Plutarch's Laconic Apothegms
Vol. I Page 406/ Published 2st. April 1781/ By
Torre No. 44 Market Lane./ [on plate, an
inscription in Greek conveying the same
meaning as the English anecdote] Engraving
6.3×6.3 plain. Friends of the Dance Collection

27 *Giovanna Baccelli*

[on plate] Signora Baccelli./ Painted by T.
Gainsborough R.A. London Pubd. According to
Act Feby. 5. 1784 by T Jones No 63 Great
Portland Street Marylebone. Engraved by
John Jones./ Mezzotint 21.1×13.5 plain.
Purchase Fund

28 *Marie Madeleine Guimard, Jean Dauberval,
and Marie Allard*

attitudes de danse éxecutées a L'Opera/ par le
Sr. Doberval et Mlles Guimard et Allard en
1779/ Dessinées et gravées par P. Lelu peintre/
a Paris chez l'Auteur Rue du Faubourg Mont
Martre No. 17/ [n d] Etching 7.1×9 plain.
Purchase Fund

29 *King's Theatre in the Haymarket*

Opera House./ London. Pub. 1st March 1809,
at R Ackermann's Repository of Arts 101
Strand./ Rowlandson & Pugin delt. et sculpt.
J. Bluck aquat./ Aquatint 7.12×9.14 colored.
Lincoln Kirstein Collection

30 *Duport's symbolic conquest of Vestris*

Frontispiece to: La Danse,/ ou/ Les Dieux de
l'Opéra,/ poëme,/ par J. Berchoux./ A Paris,/
chez Giguet et Michaud, Imp.-Libraires,/ rue
des Bons-Enfans, No. 34./ M.DCCC.VI./
15 cm. Lincoln Kirstein Collection

31 *Mademoiselle Parisot*

Mademoiselle Parisot/ London Published as the
Act directs March 11 1797 by A W Devis/
Painted by A W Devis/ Engraved by I R Smith
Messotint Engraver to his Royal Highness the
Prince of Wales/ Mezzotint 23.1×14.2 plain.
Friends of the Dance Collection

32 *Scene from a ballet by Viganò, 1812*

Rupi e scoscesi scogli che si estendono sino al
mare formando una rada capace di varj grossi
vascelli. di fianco si apre/ l'ingresso ad una vasta
ed oscura spelonca./ Questa scena fu eseguita
pel Ballo tragico L'alunno della giumenta,
ossia l'Ippotoo vendicato, composta e diretto
dal Sig. Salvatore Viganò per l'I.R. Teatro alla
Scala/ La Primavera dell'Anno 1812/ Milano,
Antonio Bossi Editore/ A. Sanquirico inv. e dip.
Carolina Lose inc./ Etching and aquatint with
wash 10.12×14.12. Cia Fornaroli Collection

33 *Pierre Gardel*

Mr. Gardel le Jeune,/ de l'Académie Royale de
Musique./ Dutertre pinx. Carrée Sculp./ [n d]
Aquatint 5.3×3.7 colored. Cia Fornaroli
Collection

34 *Marie Gardel*

Galerie Théâtrale./ 17.me Liv.on No. 66./
Coeuré del. Déposé à la Direction de la Lib.ie
Prud'hon Sculpt./ (Académie R.le de Musique.)
Mme. Gardel. (Rôle de Psyché)/ Ballet de
Psyché./ Ecrit pas Beaublé Imprimé par
Langlois/ [n d] stipple engraving 7.8.×5.15
colored. Purchase Fund

35 *A French dancing school*

[no title, n d] Drawing, pen and ink with wash
7.8×11.10 [Drawing for a colored engraving,
"Academie et Salle de Danse. Les Graces
Parisiennes," which is also in the Dance
Collection]. Purchase Fund

36 *Four couples dancing a quadrille*

L'Eté./ Lebas sculpt./ [on plate:] E/. [n d]
Engraving 5.4×7.7 colored. [One of a series of
four uniform prints, the others being: La
Pastourelle. La Poule. A droite sur les Côtés].
Purchase Fund

37 *Ballet positions from Blasis' Treatise, 1820*

Engraved illustration to: Traité Elémentaire,
théorique et pratique/ de l'Art de la Danse/ . . .
Par Ch. Blasis/ premier danseur./ Milan, 1820./
Chez Joseph Beati et Antoine Tenenti,/ Rue de
S. Marguerite (contr. di S. Margherita), No.
1066./ Imprimerie I.I. Destefanis a S. Zeno,
N. 534./ 22 cm. Cia Fornaroli Collection

38 *Classical poses from Theleur's* Letters on
Dancing

Engraved illustration to: Letters on Dancing,/
Reducing/ This elegant and healthful Exercise/

la promenade.

la passe

La valse.

Das Böhmen.

to/ Easy Scientific Principles./ . . . by E. A. Théleur,/ . . . London:/ . . . Sherwood & Co., . . . / 1831./ 27.2 cm. Cia Fornaroli Collection

39 Amalia Brugnoli, Jean Rozier, 1823

Hr. Rozier und Dlle. Brugnoli/ im Ballett die Fee und der Ritter./ lith. Institut in Wien. I.J./ [n d] Lithograph vignette 6.2×6 colored. Cia Fornaroli Collection. From the George Chaffee Collection

40 Barrymore's Il Naufragio di La Peyrouse

Esterno di una Capanna/ Questa Scena fu eseguita pel Ballo Pantomimo serio Il Naufragio di La Peyrouse, posto sulle scene dell'I.R. Teatro alla Canobbiana, dal Sig. William Barrymore/ L'Autunno dell'anno 1825./ A. Sanquirico inv. e dip. Carolina Lose inc/ aquatint 11.5×14.5 colored. Lincoln Kirstein Collection

41 Spanish bolero

The Boleras Dance./ Rev.d Wm. Bradford del. T. Clark sculp./ [n d] Aquatint vignette 8.4×11.6 colored. Purchase Fund

42 La Sonnambula

Die Nachtwandlerinn/ Pantomimisches Ballet von Scribe und Aumer./ Haupt scene./ Scholler del. Zinke sc./ Gallerie interessanter und drolliger Scenen, 4te Jahrgang. No. 1./ [n d] Engraving 7.2×9.9 colored. Cia Fornaroli Collection

43 Scene from Jocko, the Brazilian Ape

Joko, der brasilianische Affe./ Ballet von Taglioni./ Scene des glücklichen Wiedersehens./ Schoeller del. Zincke sc./ Gallerie drolliger Scenen 17.t Lieferung./ [n d] Engraving 6.15×9.14 colored. Cia Fornaroli Collection

44, 45, 46, 47 The Dancing Lesson, *four caricatures by George Cruikshank*

44 [on plate:] The 1st Position/ The Dancing Lesson- Pt. 1./ Etch.d by G. Cruik-k Pub.d by Tho.s McLean 26 Haymarket/ Aug.t 1st 1835/ Etching 4.11×6.3 plain
45 [on plate:] The Minuet./ The Dancing Lesson- Pt: 2./G. Crikshank fect- Pub.d by Thos McLean 26 Haymarket./ Aug.t 1st 1835./ Etching 4.12×6.3 plain
46 [on plate:] L'Ete/ The Dancing Lesson. Pt. 3/ G. Crikshank fec.t- Pub.d by Thos McLean 26 Haymarket/ Aug.t 1st 1835./ Etching

4.13×6.5 plain
47 [on plate:] The Sailors Hornpipe/ The Dancing Lesson Pt.4/ G. Cruikshank fect. Pub.d by Thos McLean 26 Haymarket/ Augt. 1st 1835./ Etching 4.12×6.5 plain. Lincoln Kirstein Collection

48 The Waltz

Le Maitre à danser/ Valse à Trois Temps./ 8./ Paris. Goupil et Vibert. boulevt. Montmartre, 15, et rue de Lancry, 7. Paris. T. Mayer, rue de la vieille Monnaie. 22./ London. Published 1st Novber. 1844, by the Anaglyphic Company, 25, Berners St. Oxford St./ Berlin. Verlag von L. Sachse et Cie./ Anais Colin, pinxt. Sorrieu, lith./ [n d] Lithograph 9.10×7.8 colored. Gift in memory of Arthur H. Franks

49 Taglioni and Mazilier in La Sylphide, *1832*

Madlle Taglioni, as La Sylphide,/ in the/ Mountain Sylph./ Painted by G. Lepaulle. Lith of E B. & E.C. Kellogg. Hartford Conn./ [n d] Lithograph 10.11×8.13 colored. Purchase Fund

50, 51, 52, 53, 54, 55 Marie Taglioni in La Sylphide *as drawn by Alfred E. Chalon in 1845*

[Portfolio with title page and six lithographs] La Sylphide./ Souvenir d'Adieu/ de/ Marie Taglioni/ par/ A.E. Chalon R.A./ Artistes Lithographes/ R.J. Lane A.R.A./ Edward Morton,/ J.S. Templeton,/ J.H. Lynch,/ T.H. Maguire,/ Londres. Septr.15, 1845, publié par J. Mitchell Libraire de sa Majesté,/ 33, Old Bond Street./ A Paris chez Goupil et Vibert Boulevard Montmartre, déposé./ imprimé par M & N Hanhart/
50 1./ Proof/ London Published September 8, 1845, by J. Mitchell, publisher to her Majesty, 33, Old Bond St./ A Paris chez Goupil et Vibert, Boulvt. Montmartre./ M & N Hanhart. Lith Imp. [on stone] A. E. Chalon R.A.   R. J. Lane A.R.A./
51 2./ [same text and format as 1] A. E. Chalon R.A.   J.S. Templeton/
52 3./ [same text and format] A.E. Chalon R.A. Edward Morton/
53 4./ [same text and format] A.E. Chalon R.A. J. H. Lynch/
54 5./ [same text and format] A.E. Chalon R.A. T. H. Maguire/
55 6./ [same text and format] A.E. Chalon R.A. R.J. Lane A.R.A./
Six lithographs, each octagonal 15.15×10.12 plain. Cia Fornaroli Collection. From the George Chaffee Collection

Masurka à l'Opéra.

56 The Celeste-Al Cabinet, *1836*

The Celeste-Al Cabinet./ Dickenson. Butler.
Cass. Jimmy O'Neal. Door Keeper. Celeste.
General Jackson. Kendal. Woodbury. Van
Buren./ . . . Published April 1836 by H. R.
Robinson 48 Cortland St. N.Y./ Entered
accordg. to Act of Congress in the Year 1836
by H. R. Robinson, in the Clerk's Office of the
District Court of the United States of the
Southern District of New York./ Lithograph
10.14×18.12 colored. Cia Fornaroli Collection

57 *Celeste as the Arab Boy*

Celeste./ as the Arab Boy./ A Sketch by William
Drummond/ [n d] Lithograph octagon
14.12×11.2 colored. Lincoln Kirstein Collection

58 *Eugenie LeComte*

Madame LeComte./ Principal Danseuse at the
Theatres Royal Paris, London, St. Petersburgh
&c./ In the Character of the Abbess, in Robert
le Diable./ Entered according to Act of Congress
in the Year 1837 by H. R. Robinson, in the
Clerk's Office of the District Court of the United
States, for the Southern District of New York/
The Prosecuted Picture. [facsimile autograph:]
H. R. Robinson./ Litho.y of H. R. Robinson,
52 Courtlandt St. N. Y./ [on stone:] E.W.C./
Lithograph vignette 11.8×10.3 colored. Cia
Fornaroli Collection. From the George Chaffee
Collection

59 The Three Graces

The Three Graces./ 416./ Lith. and Pub. by
N. Currier 152 Nassau cor. Spruce St. N. Y./
[on stone:] Taglioni. Elssler. Cerito./ [n d]
Lithograph 11.10×8.6 colored. Cia Fornaroli
Collection

60 *Cecilia McBride*

Miss McBride./ Pendleton's Lithography,
Boston./ [n d] Lithograph 11.8×8.2 plain.
Lincoln Kirstein Collection

61 *Paul and Amelie Taglioni in* La Sylphide

Mons. Paul Taglioni. Madame Taglioni./ In the
Characters of La Sylphide & James Reuben, at
the Park-Theatre, New-York, May 22d.. 1839./
Principal Dancers of the Opera House./
[Berlin, London, etc./] Lith. of H. R. Robinson,
52 Courtlandt St. N.Y./ [illegible signature on
stone: N. Sarony?] Lithograph trimmed to
8.11×13 colored. Purchase Fund

62 *Fanny Elssler in* La Volière

La Voliére- Portrait of Mademoiselle F. Elssler./
Printed by P. Gauci, 9, North Crescent,
Bedford Square. Drawn on Stone by M. Gauci,
from a drawing by J. Deffett Francis. [facsimile
signature:] Fanny Elssler/ London, August
1838, Published by Welch & Gwynne,
Printsellers to the Royal Family, 24, St. James's
Street. à Paris, chez Rittner & Goupil,
Boulivard Montmartre./ Deposé a la direction./
Proof/ Lithograph 20.6×13.6 plain. Friends of
of the Dance Collection. From the George
Chaffee Collection

63 *Fanny Cerrito in* La Sylphide

Fanny Cerrito/ nel ballo la Silfide di Cortesi/
Al Signor Bartolomeo Merelli che diede
occasione ai Milanesi/ di ammirare sulle scene
del Gran Teatro della Scala/ L'Esimia Artista/
l'autore Roberto Focosi D.D.D./ Milano Lit.
Gallina./ [on stone:] Focosi/ [n d] Lithograph
vignette 16.14×12.10 plain. Cia Fornaroli
Collection

64 *Marie Taglioni in* La Gitana, *1841*

Maria Taglioni/ nel ballo La Gitana/ del
coreografo Signor Filippo Taglioni padre della
esimia artista./ Chi vuol veder quanto inamori
e bei/ Danzar quaggiù come si danza in cielo/
S'affretti e venga a rimirar costei./ [on stone:]
Focosi/ [n d] Lithograph vignette 17×12.7
plain. Cia Fornaroli Collection

65 *Costume for Marie Taglioni in* Herta

Drawing from an album of 26 original designs in
water color and ink. Pencil title: Costumes/ de
Théatre/ Acteurs & Danseurs/ de l'Opéra/
[n d] 24.5 cm. [This page has been signed by
Marie Taglioni.] Friends of the Dance Collection

66 *Fanny Cerrito in* Alma

[no title, n d] Cerrito with Henri Desplaces
(left) and Jules Perrot (right). Unsigned water
color [probably by R. J. Hamerton] Octagon
13.8×10.12. Purchase Fund. From the George
Chaffee Collection

67 *Grisi and Perrot in* Esmeralda

Madelle. Carlotta Grisi, and Monsr. Perrot./ in
the very attractive ballet/ La Esmeralda./
Published by T. Mc.Lean, 26 Haymarket.
April. 6th. 1844./ J. Bouvier, del. Litho.
70. St. Martins Lane./ Lithograph 14.12×11.3
colored. Cia Fornaroli Collection. From the
George Chaffee Collection

Mazurka des Salons.

68 *Adele Dumilâtre as Myrtha in* Giselle, *1843*

[facsimile signature:] Adele Dumilatre/ as Myrtha./ in the ballet of Giselle./ London Published by T. McLean. 26 Haymarket. April 20 1843./ Bouvier del. Litho. at the General Establishment, 70 St. Martin's Lane./ Hexagonal lithograph 14.10×10.14 plain. Cia Fornaroli Collection

69 *Flora Fabbri in* The Devil to Pay

[facsimile signature:] Flora Fabbri/ as Mazourka in the Ballet of the/ Devil to Pay./ Paris, Goupil & Vibert, déposé/ Printed by M & N Hanhart./ J.W. Child, delt. London, Published February 10th 1846, by Messrs. Fores, 41, Piccadilly, corner of Sackville Street. J. Brandard, lith./ Lithograph 15.14×10.14 colored. Cia Fornaroli Collection

70 *Marietta Baderna, 1846*

Marietta Baderna/ Allieva de' Sigri. Conjugi Blasis professori di perfezionamento all' I.R. Academia di Ballo in Milano./ Prima Danzatrice all'I.R. Teatro alla Scala./ la Primavera del 1846./ Alcuni Ammiratori D.D./ Giuliani dis. Lit. Messaggi Cd. del Cappello 4025/ Lithograph 19.1×15.5 in an engraved decorative border 19.10×15.14 plain. Cia Fornaroli Collection

71 *Giovannina King*

Figaro Num. 3./ Galleria Artistico-Teatrale/ Giovannina King./ Focosi dis. Somariva eseg. Milano, Lit. Brison e Corbetta/ [biographical sketch follows] Milano Tip. Guglielmini/ [n d] Lithograph 9.5×8.2 in an engraved decorated border 15×11.9 plain. Cia Fornaroli Collection

72 *Amalia Ferraris*

Amalia Ferraris/ Vicenza 1853./ B. Marcovich foot. Vicenza Lit. Longo,/ [n d] Lithograph vignette 13.4×6.5 plain. Cia Fornaroli Collection

73 *A Neapolitan tarantella*

Frontispiece, colored lithograph, to: Tarantella/ Ballo Napolitano/ Disegnato da Gaetano Dura Diretto da Pasquale Chiodi/ A.S.E./ La Siga. Principessa d'Ottajano/ Duchessa di Miranda/ Federico Gatti/ D. D. D./ Litografia Gatti Vico 20: Monte Calvario No. 4./ 1834/ 20.3 cm. Purchase Fund

74 *Sofia Fuoco in a tarantella*

Sofia Fuoco/ nella/ Tarantella/ Lit. Ach. Paris, Firenze./ [on stone:] Sanesi/ [n d] Lithograph oval in floral border 11.6×8.13 colored. Cia Fornaroli Collection

75 Pas de Quatre (*Taglioni, Grisi, Cerrito, Grahn*) *1845*

Music cover, trimmed example, title lacking. [Marie Taglioni, Carlotta Grisi, Fanny Cerrito and Lucile Grahn in the Pas de Quatre, by Pugni, 1845. By and after John Brandard] Lithograph 11.1×8.12 colored. Cia Fornaroli Collection

76 *Nathalie Fitzjames*

Mlle. Nathalie Fitz-James./ Alex Lacauchie. Lith: J. Rigo et Cie./ Paris, Publié par Marchant./ [n d] Lithograph vignette 7.11×5.12 plain. Cia Fornaroli Collection

77 *Hermine Blangy in* Giselle

[no title, n d] Lithograph vignette 15.3×11.8 partly colored [untitled version of a lithograph by Charles Currier after Francis Davignon and Joseph Vollmering, of Hermine Blangy in *Giselle*]. Purchase Fund

78 *Giovanna Ciocca*

Sigra. Ciocca/ nella Andalusa (Park Theatre, New York) / Drawn by F. Davignon./ [n d] Lithograph octagon 15.9×12.6 in an engraved floral border 18×14.13 colored. Purchase Fund

79 *Harvest Dance of the Viennese children*

The Harvest Dance/ of the/ Viennoise Children./ Atwill, Publisher, 201 Broadway New York./ Lith. and Printed in Colors by Sarony & Major, 117, Fulton St. N.Y./ [n d] Music cover, lithograph 10×9.1 in a decorative floral border, colored [trimmed example]. Lincoln Kirstein Collection

80 *Redowa Polka*

Pasquale Borri/ H Frappart Fle. Ricci H Vienna/ Redowa Polka/ Girolamo Franceschini dess. Litografia die C Horegschj/ [n d] Lithograph 10.14×9 including decorative border with a medallion bust portrait of Borri, plain. Cia Fornaroli Collection

81 *Polish Dance*

Polnischer Tanz./ (Wesele w oycowie) / Berlin, F. Sala & Co. Unter d. Linden 57. Druck v. H. Waldow jun/ New York Max Jacoby & Zeller/ [n d] Lithograph 10.10×15.5 colored. Purchase Fund

82   Tarantella in L'Étoile de Messine, *1861*

Musée de Moeurs en Actions/ Scène de l'Opéra
La Tarantelle. (Étoile de Messine.)/ Peint par
Morlon Imp. Lemercier, 57, R. de Seine, Paris.
Lith. par Regnier, Bettanier, Morlon/ 8./ Paris,
Eugène Jouy, 56, Boulev'd de Sébastopol.
New-York, Emile Seitz, 413 Broadway/ [n d]
Lithograph 15.8×20.12 colored. Purchase Fund

83   The Ronzani Ballet

Ronzani's Grand Ballet Troupe/ from the
Theatre La Scala in Milan the Royal Theatre in
Turin, Her Majesty's Theatre London, Academy
of Music Philadelphia/ lith. by B. F. Smith. Jr.
N.Y. Printed in tints, by F. Michelin. 169
Broadway. N.Y./ [n d] Lithograph 18.15×25.11
colored. Cia Fornaroli Collection. From the
George Chaffee Collection

Mazurka des Salons

Mazurka Nationale

Page 1   Fritellino

Engraved illustration to: Bernard Picart:
Titulus Stultorum. [Amsterdam, 1696.
Manuscript title: Commedia dell'Arte/ 12
Figures./ 1720. C del A./ 15/] 19.6 cm. From
the library of Gordon Craig

Pages 80–86   Vignettes from

La Polka./ Paris (Mon Aumont) François
Delarue Succ. rue J.J. Rousseau, 10 Imp.
Lemercier. London, pub. 20 October by the
Anaglyphic Company, 25 Berners St. Oxford
St./ [9 vignettes titled: La promenade, La valse,
La valse roulée, Pas Bohémien, La poursuite,
Le dos à dos, Le moulinet, Pas Bohémien en
valsant, La passe. n d] Lithograph 15.11×13.4
colored. Purchase Fund

and

La Mazurka./ Paris (Mon Aumont) François
Delarue Succ, rue J.J. Rousseau, 10. Imp.
Lemercier. London- pub. 10 November by the
Anaglyphic Company, 25 Berners St. Oxford
St./ [3 vignettes titled: Mazurka à l'Opéra,
3 titled: Mazurka des Salons, 3 titled: Mazurka
Nationale. n d] Lithograph 15.12×13.4 colored.
Purchase Fund

Cover paper motifs adapted from

Le Rigaudon de la paix (plates 4–7) engraved
illustrations to: Choregraphie/ ou/ l'Art de
De'crire/ La Dance,/ par Caracteres, Figures/
et Signes De'monstratifs,/ . . . Par M. Feuillet,
Maître de Dance./ A Paris,/ Chez l'Auteur . . ./
Et chez Michel Brunet . . ./ M.DCC./ Avec
Privilege du Roy./ 23.8 cm. Lincoln Kirstein
Collection

Mazurka à l'Opéra

Mazurka à l'Opéra

la valse roulée

This Book, designed by Bert Waggott, was set in Monotype and foundry Bulmer by The Stinehour Press, Lunenburg, Vermont. Offset printing was done by The Meriden Gravure Company, Meriden, Connecticut, on Mohawk Superfine Text supplied by Lindenmeyr Schlosser Paper Company. Binding was done by Russell-Rutter Company, Inc., New York.